WELCOME TO THE
WILLIAMSBURG INN

"Careful, brooding study of every detail of a bedroom, particularly when small, is in my experience the only way in which to get a completely satisfying result . . . I shall not be happy to go forward with the Williamsburg Inn until I feel that the most possible has been made of each room as regards comfort, convenience and charm."

John D. Rockefeller, Jr.

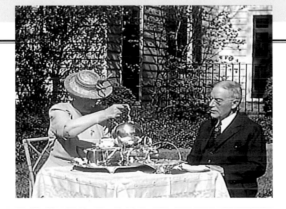

WELCOME TO THE WILLIAMSBURG INN

BY HUGH DESAMPER

PHOTOGRAPHY BY TOM GREEN

ADDITIONAL PHOTOGRAPHY BY BILL BOXER, DAVID M. DOODY,
MIKE KLEMME, JEFF MCNAMARA, LISA MASSON,
MICHAEL WAINE, JOHN WHITEHEAD, AND THE STAFF
OF THE COLONIAL WILLIAMSBURG FOUNDATION

Published by The Colonial Williamsburg Foundation
Williamsburg, Virginia
In Association with
LICKLE PUBLISHING INC

Photos on pages 30-31, 42-43, 44 (left), 73, 91, and 96-97 © 1997 by Bill Boxer

Photos on frontispiece, pages 23, 46, 47, 48, 49 (above), 50-51, 51 (below), 52-53, 59, and back cover © 1997 by Jeff McNamara

Photos on pages 55, 56, 57, 58, 60, and 61 © 1997 by Michael Waine

DeSamper, Hugh.
    Welcome to the Williamsburg Inn / Hugh DeSamper : photography
by Bill Boxer . . . [et al.] and the staff of the Colonial Williamsburg
Foundation.
      p. cm
    ISBN 0-87935-160-1 (C. W.)
    ISBN 1-890674-04-4 (Lickle)
    I. Williamsburg Inn (Williamsburg, Va.)—History. I. Colonial
Williamsburg Foundation. II. Title.
TX941.W53W45 1997
647.94755'425201--DC21   97-10002
                                      CIP

Book design by Joel Avirom

Printed in Canada

*T*he Williamsburg Inn has served for sixty years as a place of beauty, rest, and relaxation for visitors to Colonial Williamsburg, who come to experience the special place where America's democratic ideals and values were won.

The Williamsburg Inn has become a destination renowned for its hospitality, its cuisine, and its recreational facilities. Today, it plays host to celebrities, heads of state, dignitaries, and guests from around the world. The Inn continues to be a home away from home for travelers, offering them the finest of amenities and service.

The Williamsburg Inn, one of the Official Resort Hotels of Colonial Williamsburg, is operated by Colonial Williamsburg Hotel Properties, Inc., a subsidiary of the Colonial Williamsburg Foundation. Revenues support the preservation of the eighteenth-century capital of Virginia and Colonial Williamsburg's educational mission.

A warm welcome always awaits you at the Williamsburg Inn.

ROBERT C. WILBURN, PRESIDENT
THE COLONIAL WILLIAMSBURG FOUNDATION

*T*he historic and gracious Williamsburg Inn reminds guests of the pleasures of a Virginia country estate. The Inn enjoys a reputation for the finest in gourmet dining, elegant accommodations, and attentive service. Complete resort facilities include world-class golf, tennis courts, swimming pools, lawn bowling, and beautifully landscaped grounds designed to please the most discriminating of travelers. The Williamsburg Inn is committed to ensuring that every guest experiences the warmth and care for which it has been recognized both nationally and internationally.

The story of how the Williamsburg Inn came to be built began more than seventy years ago. In 1926, Dr. W. A. R. Goodwin convinced John D. Rockefeller, Jr., to undertake the restoration of Virginia's colonial capital. As the work progressed, the Reverend Goodwin observed: "Many visitors, having heard that the colonial city was to be restored, assumed that within twelve months it would surely be finished. They began to arrive. No suitable place had yet been provided for their accommodation."

Dr. W. A. R. Goodwin, engineer Robert Trimble, John D. Rockefeller, Jr., and landscape architect Arthur A. Shurcliff (left to right) consult over blueprints.

To house those who wished to remain overnight, Colonial Williamsburg acquired the twentieth-century Colonial Inn located on Market Square where Chowning's Tavern now stands. The refurbished hostelry reopened as the Williamsburg Inn in 1931. Since it contained only twenty-one rooms, planners quickly realized that the Colonial Inn would not be a long-term solution to the problem of where to accommodate large numbers of overnight guests. Furthermore, the Colonial Inn was also unsuitable

because no one wanted to retain a twentieth-century building in the heart of the Historic Area.

Some suggested using the Raleigh Tavern as a hotel. Intriguing at first, this idea was soon abandoned and the Raleigh opened as an exhibition building. Other planners proposed adapting an additional colonial building to use as lodgings. The concept gained support, and Market Square Tavern also opened for guests in 1931.

Plans for constructing a new, high-quality hotel with ample rooms for the ever-increasing number of visitors continued to be discussed, however. The major stumbling block was the choice of a site since building the new hotel on Duke of Gloucester Street would conflict with the decision to restore the Historic Area to the way it had looked in the eighteenth century.

At the same time, a consulting firm recommended that Colonial Williamsburg incorporate in the development of the Inn a wide variety of recreational amenities found at leading American resorts. Creating a complete, self-contained resort as a destination for guests became the goal of Colonial Williamsburg Hotel Properties.

In 1935, planners selected a location on the south side of Francis Street just beyond the boundary of the Historic Area. The choice pleased those who championed the historic preservation point of view. It also met the practical needs expressed by the Hotel Properties group.

BELOW: *A still unpaved road leads to the Williamsburg Inn. The complex was completed just in time for the grand opening in April 1937.*

OPPOSITE: *Townspeople recalled that workers planted many large trees on the grounds of the Inn.*

2

OLD SWEET

Architect William G. Perry believed it was essential to choose an architectural style for the new Inn that would set it apart from the look of the restored eighteenth-century town. Perry explained, "It was considered appropriate to adopt a style that is at the same time Virginian and extra-18th Century."

Virginia had long been known for its heated mineral springs. People flocked to "take the waters," which they believed could cure any number of illnesses. Sweet Springs, an old favorite in Monroe County, West Virginia, about a mile beyond the modern Virginia border, provided the greatest inspiration for the Williamsburg Inn. Not one "of these Springs Hotels is more pleasing in character than . . . the Old Sweet," Perry said. Its buildings are "so pleasantly suggestive that, more than any other, they were used as a guide to the character of the new Inn at Williamsburg."

Construction of the Inn began in April 1936. The building took shape rapidly to meet the deadline set for a spring 1937 opening.

In April editorials, the local *Virginia Gazette* praised the Foundation for building "such a magnificent hostelry. The increasing number of tourists and visitors to Williamsburg each day makes more hotel accommodations necessary." The newspaper predicted: "Before the new hotel is completed, another addition will be necessary, with enough bedrooms to take care of at least four hundred or more people . . . With spring's arrival, the rush of tourists has been unprecedented, as many as fifteen bus loads in a day . . . hundreds of foreign cars can be seen from every state of the union as well as from Canada."

Early the next year, the *Gazette* recounted, "The kitchen is a marvel of utility . . . Gadgets here and gadgets there, give promise of quick and efficient service in the dining rooms . . . Extensive landscaping is under way with workmen moving hundreds of yards of dirt, at times

Second Section   Second Section

THE

VIRGINIA GAZETTE.

Containing the freſheſt Advices, Foreign and Domeſtick.

(Founded 1736)

NEW SERIES—VOL. VIII, NO. 14   WILLIAMSBURG, VIRGINIA, FRIDAY, APRIL 2, 1937   SINGLE COPY—FIVE CENTS

FINE NEW WILLIAMSBURG INN TO BE OPENED TOMORROW

*"Fine New
Williamsburg Inn
To Be Opened
Tomorrow"
heralded the* Gazette.
*The newspaper noted
that "Williamsburg's
$750,000 Inn Will
Be Formally Opened
on Saturday With
Host of Important
Persons Present."*

working into the night and on Sundays. Many large trees have been transported to the property."

The number of visitors continued to increase. "Clubs and school groups, and individuals with a history hobby, have been making serious pilgrimages to Williamsburg for some time," *Hotel Monthly* reported. "This year the tourist rush started earlier than usual, and since March 26 an average of a thousand visitors a day have entered the town."

The Inn had the honor of hosting the Williamsburg Rotary Club at a preview dinner on March 26. The American Institute of Decorators, the first conference to meet there, convened for four days just before the official opening to view the architecture and decor and enjoy the facilities, grounds, and cuisine.

A sunny day graced the grand opening on April 3, 1937. The following week, a *Gazette* editorial noted that those who had visited the new Inn "have only the highest praise for this fine addition . . . we have yet to hear of anything

WELCOME . . . SHIRLEY TEMPLE

Shirley Temple, the film darling of the thirties, was a guest at the Inn on June 30, 1938. The *Gazette* reported: "She was her own natural, charming self while being conducted through the [Governor's Palace], expressing keen interest in everything. Told that the Governor and his lady frequently sat on the balcony overlooking the Palace Green, she expressed a desire to go out. Getting permission, she called to the large crowd of young and old who had gathered from all parts of the city to see her."

Shirley Temple Black, who later served as U. S. Chief of Protocol and was ambassador to Ghana, visited the Inn again as an adult.

4

like it anywhere, not even in Europe." The newspaper predicted that the Inn would become a well-known resort for tourists who came to see Williamsburg.

Miss Mary Lindsley, formerly the manager of a prestigious hotel in Washington, D. C., came to Williamsburg to direct the operations of the Inn. After Miss Lindsley helped plan the new facility, guided it through construction, and arranged the opening, she fell ill and found it necessary to resign.

John D. Green assumed Miss Lindsley's responsibilities in June 1937. Kenneth Chorley, president of Colonial Williamsburg, wrote to Green advising him that "whenever Mr. and Mrs. Rockefeller move into a new home, they stay in every guest room before they move into the master bedroom. There are 61 rooms in the Inn. You have two months before your family [the Rockefellers] arrives." Today, the Williamsburg Inn continues the long-standing tradition of treating guests who stay there as "family."

The World War II years offered new challenges to the Williamsburg Inn. Gasoline had become tightly rationed by the spring of 1942. For average Americans, driving was limited to an occasional visit to the grocery store or other essential trips. Since 98 percent of the guests at the Inn arrived by car, gas rationing meant that the occupancy rate plummeted.

General manager Green later recalled the ways in which the Inn contributed to the war effort: "What to do with an empty hotel? After consultation with the military, it was decided to offer accommodations in the Inn exclusively to officers permanently stationed in the area on a non-profit basis as an aid to the war effort. These officers were in the Williamsburg area to train the thousands of draftees at nearby Fort Eustis and Camp Peary. Rates

This attractive room is an example of the Rockefellers' determination that the Inn should be as unlike a hotel as possible. A painting from Mrs. Rockefeller's celebrated collection of American folk art hangs over the fireplace.

WELCOME . . . THE BRITISH GENERAL STAFF

In May 1943, the Inn received a request to make the hotel available as a top secret weekend retreat for the British General Staff who would be in Washington for important consultations.

The allies landed at Langley Air Force Base. Vernon M. Geddy, Sr., executive vice president of Colonial Williamsburg, went with the motorcade to greet the group and escort them to Williamsburg. The most direct route to the Inn went past the Yorktown battlefield. Geddy hoped they could pass it without any comment. However, the British officers quickly took note of the many redoubts and fortifications in the area. General Sir Alan Brooke, the chief of the Imperial General Staff, asked what they were.

"This is Yorktown, sir," Geddy replied.

After a rather lengthy silence, the general looked at him humorously and asked, "I say, Mr. Geddy. Who was that chap of ours who did so badly here?"

were fixed at . . . $2 single and $3 double per day, and the Inn enjoyed an occupancy of 100 per cent for the duration."

More and more people went to work in the local defense industry as the war continued, so help was in short supply. As a result, the Inn decided to close the dining room and kitchen.

In February 1946, nearly four years after the facility closed for general use, the Williamsburg Inn reopened to the "civilian public."

General Dwight D. Eisenhower escorted Winston Churchill to Williamsburg on March 8, 1946. The statesman had just given his famous "Iron Curtain" speech at Westminster College and then had addressed a joint session of the Virginia General Assembly in Richmond.

Churchill was well known for his sense of humor. He commented to his hosts, Mr. and Mrs. John D. Rockefeller 3rd, "Very interesting. In our country we number kings. You number Rockefellers."

During Churchill's visit, the British Union Jack, the Stars and Stripes, and the Virginia state flag fluttered together over the entrance to the Inn.

OPPOSITE: *Abby Aldrich and John D. Rockefeller, Jr., and other representatives of the Foundation greet military guests.*
RIGHT: *Churchill and Eisenhower share a joke and a drink during the former British prime minister's visit in 1946.*

*A*n automobile turns into the oval drive that leads to the Williamsburg Inn. Ahead, tall portico columns and a line of arches accent a rambling, whitewashed, brick mansion enhanced by lanterns and topiary plantings. The feeling is one of elegance and well being. The passengers are greeted by a smiling bellman. "Welcome to the Williamsburg Inn," he says.

Guests step into a bright, airy, oversize living room with a fireplace at each end. Opposite the entryway, handsome arched French doors open onto a flagstone terrace that overlooks meticulously groomed grounds. Flowers and shrubs in unusual combinations flourish everywhere. The beauty of southern favorites—dogwoods, azaleas, and magnolias—is complemented by boxwoods, poet's laurel, several varieties of hollies, aucubas, viburnums, and emerald and gold euonymus, among other flora.

Mr. and Mrs. John D. Rockefeller, Jr., were involved in every aspect of the design, construction, and furnishing of the Inn. Determined that the facility would be unlike a hotel, the Rockefellers chose to create the atmosphere of a comfortable private home where they would be proud to bring their own guests. They decided the Inn should be decorated in the Regency style of early nineteenth-century England to set it apart from the decor characteristic of the Georgian period that is appropriate in the Historic Area.

In the public spaces, the Regency style is seen in neoclassical architectural features such as interior cornices, chair rails, and window muntins, and in the templelike sculpture of the pediments, arches, and columns. In furnishings, Regency followed the architectural trend from heaviness to lightness, and from carved surfaces to flat surfaces with inlaid or painted decoration. Luxurious fabrics are used throughout the Inn

OPPOSITE: *The reproduction portrait over the mantel is of Henry St. George Tucker, circa 1841, attributed to William J. Hubard. Generations of Tuckers contributed to the legal and cultural life of Williamsburg.*
OVERLEAF: *Crimson upholstery and custom-designed draperies and trimmings create a warm, inviting ambience in the lobby. Crystal prisms on the Regency-style chandelier catch the light.*

Mrs. Rockefeller supervised the placement of the furniture in the original lobby. The arrangement has not changed over the years.

The oval rug in the lobby is a precise replica of the original that John D. and Abby Aldrich Rockefeller purchased before the Inn opened. When the rug began to show signs of wear, a staff designer photographed it, traced a scale pattern of each decorative motif, and clipped fibers to ensure exact color reproduction. These design elements were sent to China where another hand-hooked copy was produced in nine months. The same design is seen in the lobby today.

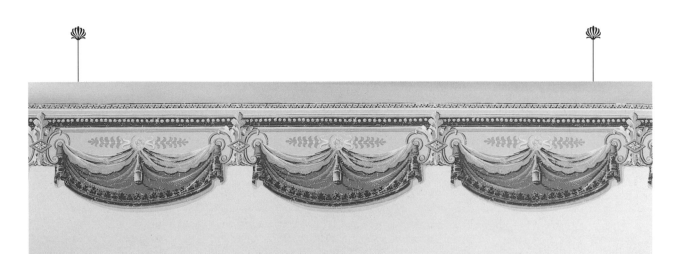

Mr. and Mrs. Rockefeller paid great attention to every detail, even the most minute. One morning, dissatisfied with the appearance of the lobby, Mrs. Rockefeller asked helpers to rearrange the furniture to make the space more inviting. She supervised the project—which took several hours—until the furniture and accessories had been placed just as she wished. The furniture still remains as Mrs. Rockefeller arranged it.

Along the hallways and corridors of the Inn is an interesting collection of artworks, among them old prints and drawings that depict vistas of England and Europe. The public rooms contain oil paintings of family groups and individuals from the past. The carpet in the hallways is a custom design that features the Williamsburg Inn's logo, which was developed before the facility opened.

Mr. and Mrs. Rockefeller approved the decorative schemes of every bedroom at the Inn. The neoclassical design of each creates the atmosphere of an English country home. Classic wall coverings, silk draperies, exquisite fabrics, and late eighteenth- and nineteenth-century prints and paintings complement the antique and reproduction Regency furniture.

ABOVE: *This ceiling border highlights the hallways in the main part of the Inn. It is documented in a nineteenth-century design book.*
LEFT: *Two large convex Federal mirrors flank the opposite ends of the lobby.*
BELOW LEFT: *A crane devouring a pomegranate and cluster of grapes is depicted on this Regency sconce.*

Inspired by a Regency source, a custom-made gray carpet with rosettes and the same design and colors has been used here since the Inn opened.

OPPOSITE: *An elegant Federal desk and bookcase houses nineteenth-century ceramics.*
LEFT: *A yellow floral motif accents an English porcelain hand-painted plate.*
BELOW LEFT: *English ornithologist John Gould rendered this painting of birds, one of many that hang throughout the Inn.*
BELOW RIGHT: *The portrait of an eighteenth-century family is by an unknown artist.*
RIGHT: *A nineteenth-century tall clock of exceptional quality was a gift to the Inn from a guest.*

Adams-style wallcoverings and draperies accent the sunny card room.

RIGHT: *Families come to the Williamsburg Inn to relax and reunite.*

OPPOSITE: *A perfect day begins with a leisurely breakfast from room service and the morning newspaper.*

OVERLEAF: *Gilt cornice boards over peacock blue silk damask draperies, gilt on cream wallpaper, and a gilt mirror reinforce the classical theme.*

From the beginning, the Williamsburg Inn's premier policy has been to treat every guest like a king or queen. Over the years, the Inn has been a home-away-from-home for guests of all ages and from every continent. The staff takes pride in anticipating every request and making each visit unforgettable. People who stay at the Inn feel it truly is their home. Archives filled with testimonials to the Inn and its people explain why so many guests come back again and again to enjoy its "wonderful hospitality," "impeccable, courteous service," and "caring staff."

WELCOME . . .
THE EMPEROR AND EMPRESS OF JAPAN

Emperor Hirohito and Empress Nagato of Japan made their first trip abroad in November 1975. The Williamsburg Inn was one of their stops in America.

In preparation for their visit, upholsterers were asked to refit a horse-drawn carriage with bulletproof material. They took the vehicle apart piece by piece, installed the protective material, and reassembled each part so "even the Secret Service couldn't tell it had been altered." The carriage is still in use.

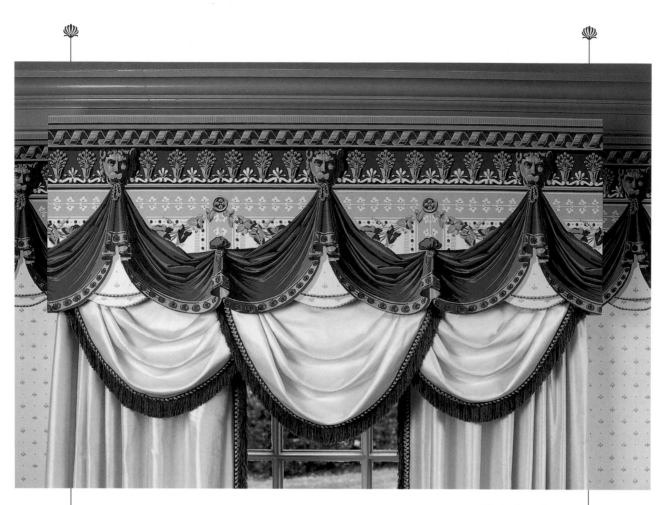

ABOVE AND OPPOSITE: *Underhanging festoons of white silk accented with green echo the accurate Regency border and wall treatment in this lovely bedroom.*

WELCOME . . . THE McDONNELLS

Jim and Nancy McDonnell of Boardman, Ohio, have made more than one hundred trips to Williamsburg together. "The memories began with our honeymoon here in

May 1966," Mrs. McDonnell said. "It was our first time at the Inn, and we couldn't have had a more delightful visit." They came back that December for the holidays and have returned every Christmas for thirty years.

"The people here make it so special," Mr. McDonnell added. "The five stars of the Inn don't matter a bit to us. The managers and their entire staff are the stars. Colonial Williamsburg should be proud."

OPPOSITE: *The fleurette design of the pale green silk draperies replicates the original nineteenth-century textile in the Colonial Williamsburg collections. The Federal gaming table and easy chair are exact reproductions of the antiques.*

WELCOME . . . THE MAHERS

Bill and Mary Maher of Linden, Virginia, have been coming to Williamsburg since 1960, spending an average of six weeks each year.

The couple met in college while studying for master's degrees. Soon after their marriage, they began to take trips to Williamsburg. Mrs. Maher, an interior designer, has incorporated the Williamsburg look into their own home. She explains, "We concentrate on furniture and other decorative features (collected mostly on our many visits) in one room which we refer to as 'our Williamsburg room.'"

The Mahers also visit other resorts during the year. "But we tell them how you do it at the Inn," Mrs. Maher said. "The service, and the way the staff remembers names, and the friendliness that we always see. It's the little things—like 'our' table on Saturday nights in the Regency Dining Room—that make the Inn so special."

Formal yet comfortable and inviting, a typical bed-sitting suite reflects the classicism found throughout the Inn.

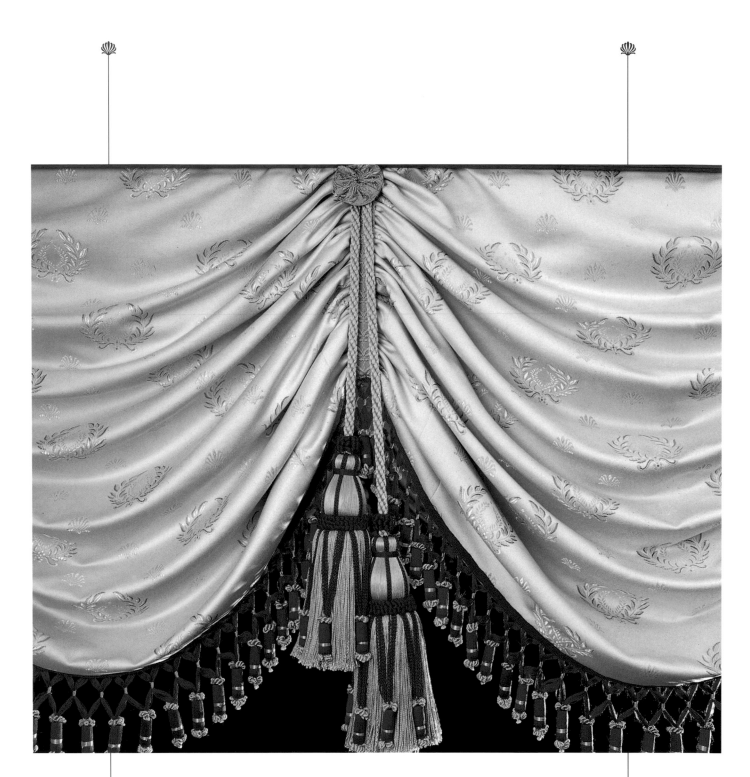

ABOVE: *Detail of the hand-made silk tassels and trim on the canopy. The fabric is a cream-colored silk sateen.*

OPPOSITE: *Custom-made, hand-blocked wallpaper duplicates a Regency design. A Wilton carpet covers the floor.*

OPPOSITE: *The sophisticated early nineteenth-century design of the curtains is taken from an English country house with Regency interiors. A multi-colored floral silk is used on the windows and oversize twin beds in this guest room.*

ABOVE RIGHT: *A nineteenth-century-style dressing table with matching trifold mirror and bench is original to the Inn. Pieces such as these are still found in most guest rooms.*

ABOVE: *NATO Defense Ministers.*
RIGHT: *President and Mrs. Ronald Reagan.*
OPPOSITE: *Eight world leaders came to Williamsburg to participate in the Economic Summit in 1983.*

*T*he Williamsburg Inn offers international dignitaries a discreet hideaway where they can prepare for meetings with government leaders in Washington, D. C. Over the years, the Inn has welcomed many heads of state and has extended hospitality to a number of important national and international meetings, thus carrying on a tradition that began nearly three centuries ago when statesmen first gathered in Williamsburg to debate and formulate policy.

The 1983 Economic Summit convened in Williamsburg by President Ronald Reagan brought eight world leaders to the Inn. Present for deliberations were Prime Minister Pierre Trudeau of Canada, President Gaston Thorn of the European Community, Chancellor Helmut Kohl of Germany, President François Mitterrand of France, Prime Minister Yasuhiro Nakasone of Japan, Prime Minister Margaret Thatcher of Great Britain, and Prime Minister Amintore Fanfani of Italy.

Other noteworthy groups that have stayed at the Inn include the NATO Defense Ministers, social and cultural emissaries from many nations, and members of the Academy of Achievement. The Inn has also hosted celebrity visitors from the world of entertainment, including Bill Cosby, Naomi Judd, and Tom Selleck, to name just a few.

37

Queen Elizabeth II and Prince Philip will forever be identified with the East Wing of the Williamsburg Inn. The royal couple came to Williamsburg on October 16, 1957, in honor of the 350th anniversary of the settlement at Jamestown in 1607. Her Majesty and the prince consort stayed in the second-floor suite now referred to as "The Queen's Suite."

Wearing a diamond tiara and a glistening white satin gown embroidered with precious and semi-precious stones, Queen Elizabeth descended the sweeping curved staircase in the East Wing on her way to dinner that evening.

Bellman Nat Reid remembers the occasion well: "What made it so beautiful is that she is such a gracious lady, which you knew she would be, and she was so appreciative of every little thing the help did for her . . . She would smile every time she came by you. Ask anyone who was here and they invariably remember the smile, the graciousness, and the way she received and accepted the help."

Dinner Menu for
Queen Elizabeth and Prince Philip

Colonial Williamsburg's dinner in honor of the queen and the prince consort was planned very carefully. From discreet inquiries, planners learned about the royal couple's preferences. Menus for the preceding and following days were considered as well. The festive dinner featured the following dishes:

Clear Green Turtle Soup, Amontillado
Cheese Straws

Mushrooms Bordelaise

Williams and Humbert Dry Sack

——

Boneless Breast of Chicken with Virginia Ham

Baby Green Beans, Amandine

Bâtard Montrachet, 1953

——

Avocado Slices
French Dressing

——

Fresh Strawberry Mousse

Veuve Clicquot Yellow Label, Dry

——

Demitasse and Liqueurs

MARY REDCROSS

Mary Redcross worked in housekeeping at the Inn for thirty-two years. She prepared the rooms for Queen Elizabeth II and Prince Philip in 1957, and for the Emperor and Empress of Japan in 1975. Guests appreciated Mary's hospitality and often asked for her whenever they stayed at the Inn.

Mary explained that king-size beds created a problem for her. "I'm not quite five feet tall, so I had to lay flat out on one side to make half of it, then crawl all the way across to finish."

The spacious, sunny public room of the East Lounge is particularly appealing. Here, couples and families gather to read, enjoy a game of cards, or refresh themselves with afternoon tea and cookies accompanied by relaxing piano music.

A tremendous amount of effort ensures that every visit to the Williamsburg Inn is special. The staff polish furniture and brass, sweep sidewalks, arrange flowers, order, prepare, and cook food, wash dishes and put them away, turn down beds and place a chocolate just so, and on and on.

Ongoing maintenance and room refurbishment are essential to maintain the Inn's high standards. Unseen by guests but essential to its operations, seamstresses, interior designers, painters, carpenters, flower arrangers, and engineers strive to ensure that each visitor's sojourn at the Inn is enjoyable. Guests often ask for a glimpse of "behind-the-scenes" activities, and the Inn staff is delighted to escort them on a tour of the heart of the hotel.

OVERLEAF: *Teas, weddings, receptions, and other memorable events occur in the East Lounge.*

Lovely candelabra with a Grecian motif adorn the classical-style mantel in the East Lounge.

NAT REID

Head bellman Nat Reid was entered in the American Hotel & Motel Association's annual Bellman of the Year contest by the Inn manager. To the delight of everyone at the Inn, Reid won. He was chosen from the more than sixty thousand bellmen in the United States, Canada, Mexico, and the Caribbean who were nominated.

The president of the AH&MA introduced Reid as "more than the best bellman; he is a symbol of devotion to service and excellence of every bellman." Reid accepted the award, noting that "it is the bellman who makes the first impression on a guest. You've got to make them feel at home when they cross your door. It doesn't end there, either. You are supposed to try to anticipate their wants and needs."

THESSALONIANS JUDKINS

Thessalonians Judkins, room service captain extraordinaire, came to work in 1938 and remained at the Inn for forty-seven years. He is shown welcoming President and Mrs. Richard Nixon on one of their visits to Williamsburg.

ABOVE LEFT: *Lady Sarah Howard.*
ABOVE RIGHT: *Mr. and Mrs. Rockefeller traveled to the Continent to select artwork and accessories for the Inn. In England, they purchased the pair of mirrors that hang outside the East Lounge.*

*T*he formal lower dining room, which accommodates 184, was added in 1972. Elements of the royal pavilion at Brighton, England, built for the Prince of Wales (later George IV) by John Nash, inspired the period style of the Regency Dining Room. Palm-leaved columns, gleaming crystal chandeliers, silk draperies, and leather-upholstered furniture create a beautiful setting for a special dining experience. The walls are adorned with hand-painted oriental panels whose tree of life design features peonies and birds reminiscent of the rooms in the Brighton Pavilion.

A glassed-in walkway with attractive views of the Inn's exterior connects the Regency Room with the original dining room. The upper dining room was modified to serve as a reception area and more intimate space for meals when the Regency Room was built.

Breakfast, brunch, lunch, afternoon tea, dinner, and evening refreshments are offered in the elegant Regency Lounge. Antique framed Chinese silk panels and seventeenth-century Coromandel screens selected by Mr. and Mrs. Rockefeller grace the room. Mrs. Rockefeller also chose the Regency carpet, whose design has never changed over the years.

Hans Schadler, C.E.C, A.A.C., is the executive chef and head of the culinary department at the Inn. On the busiest days, the chef and his sixty-member team prepare meals for as many as twelve hundred diners. When Chef Schadler describes the cuisine at the Inn, he comments, "I call it classical cooking with regional and seasonal influences. I try to keep it balanced."

OPPOSITE: *The Regency Dining Room emulates the style of the Brighton Pavilion in England. Leonidas and Sari roses in shades of rust and orange and green bells of Ireland enhance the floral arrangement.*
BELOW: *Hand-painted silk Chinese wallpaper panels embellish the dining room.*

OPPOSITE: *The door with its charming bell canopy is an exact copy of one in the Brighton Pavilion.*
LEFT: *A glass gallery connects the Regency Dining Room with the upper dining room. Everlastings on the Regency pier table include peonies, roses, larkspurs, artemisia, and globe thistles. Urns of grape ivy are used for accent.*
BELOW: *The bird bath outside the glass gallery is popular with feathered guests.*

OPPOSITE: *The upper dining room.*
ABOVE: *Gilt highlights a detail on a classical Corinthian column.*
CENTER: *Fluted, hand-blown glass was used to create a beautiful ceiling fixture.*
BELOW: *Mr. Rockefeller presented these pieces from his important collection of Chinese export porcelain to the Inn.*

LEFT: *Featured in this buffet served in the Regency Lounge are steamed clams and mussels, five-nut chutney, cherry tomatoes and fresh asparagus, roast turkey, and Virginia ham, a longtime southern favorite.*
BELOW: *Chef Schadler adds a finishing touch.*

Chef Crawford and Winston Churchill

Chef Fred Crawford came to the Williamsburg Inn soon after it opened in 1936. He established the Inn's reputation for fine cuisine that was based primarily on traditional southern cooking.

Sir Winston Churchill was an admirer of Chef Crawford. When the statesman visited Williamsburg in 1946, he was so taken with the Clear Green Turtle Soup, Amontillado served at the dinner in his honor that he requested more. Before departing for the nation's capital later that evening, Churchill asked if he could have yet another plate of turtle soup. Although the kitchen had closed, Chef Crawford was still in the building and quickly sent a tureen of soup to Sir Winston's room.

Well-known food authority Craig Claiborne described Chef Crawford's Sunday Night Buffet as "the most lavish buffet on the East Coast."

OPPOSITE: *Iced oysters, clams, crabmeat, and shrimp are accompanied by traditional cocktail sauce, oyster crackers, fresh horseradish, and Tabasco sauce.*

OPPOSITE: *Delicate mixed organic baby greens are delicious in a salad.*
ABOVE: *Winter squash bisque garnished with pecan chantilly cream.*

LEFT: *Wide ribbons of pappardelle pasta tossed with fresh basil and seasonal vegetables.*
BELOW: *Horseradish cream sauce and dill top a succulent serving of steamed salmon. Asparagus, corn, roasted potatoes, Shiitake mushrooms, and fresh herbs accompany the fish.*
OPPOSITE: *Rack of lamb is a specialty of the Regency Dining Room.*

BELOW: *The Governor's chocolate torte.*
RIGHT: *Luscious desserts— pecan tart, cheesecake with mandarin oranges, blackberries, and kiwi fruit, and custard fruit tart topped with strawberries, pineapple, and kiwis—are irresistible.*

61

The world-renowned sommelier at the Inn presides over an extensive selection of imported and domestic wines. He always discusses wines with guests in order to understand their interest in wine, their personal preferences, and the entrées they have selected. This information helps the sommelier suggest a wine or wines to best enhance their meals.

ABOVE: *Mint juleps on the terrace.*
RIGHT: *Cast-iron benches with lyre backs are original to the Inn.*
OPPOSITE: *As seen from the terrace behind the East Lounge, the curve, proportions, and dentil molding of the Williamsburg Inn are reminiscent of buildings in Regency England.*

*Palladian influence is
reflected in the arched doorway
that opens onto the terrace.*

Guests step backward in time and sample life as it was lived two hundred years ago when they stay in one of the Colonial Houses. Once inhabited by citizens of eighteenth-century Williamsburg, the Colonial Houses are full of history and lore. Located just a short stroll from the Inn, the Colonial Houses enjoy all the conveniences and amenities of the Inn itself.

Market Square Tavern, an original building, has welcomed travelers since the eighteenth century. The restored hostelry, which opened in 1931 as the first colonial building available for overnight guests, now looks much as it did during its heyday. Checked and solid color fabrics in the rooms are similar to those which were there during colonial days. The blue check has been documented from an eighteenth-century textile in the Colonial Williamsburg collections. The solid colors used for the chairs and seat cushions have also been authenticated.

Among the other colonial houses available for overnight stays is the Lewis House on the corner of Francis and Colonial Streets. It, too, is decorated much as it would have been more than two centuries ago.

Linen draperies with a blue and white resist design have been taken from an original textile in the collections of Colonial Williamsburg. A handsome leather fire bucket filled with sand lends an authentic touch. "J G W" on the cradle are believed to be the initials of the child for whom it was constructed.

67

TOM JEFFERSON AT
MARKET SQUARE TAVERN

More than two hundred years ago, young Tom Jefferson rented rooms in Market Square Tavern when he was studying law under the guidance of George Wythe, the foremost legal mind of his day. Jefferson rose before sunrise each morning to complete his lessons in chemistry, anatomy, ethics, religion, botany, and other subjects. Then he hurried to Professor Wythe's home on Palace green for instruction in the law. Since no one knows which rooms Jefferson rented, every twentieth-century guest can imagine he or she is sleeping where the future third president once did.

OPPOSITE: *Market Square Tavern.*
ABOVE: *Lewis House.*
LEFT: *Lewis House bedchamber. The trunk is a copy of one associated with Thomas Jefferson.*

Across the street, The Quarter is a small nineteenth-century cottage with an attractive shed roofline. Some researchers believe it served for a time as slave quarters. Cary Grant chose The Quarter for his lodgings when the filming of *The Howards of Virginia* took place in Williamsburg in 1940.

A few doors east is the Bracken Tenement, once owned by the Reverend John Bracken. He was rector of Bruton Parish Church for forty-five years, mayor of Williamsburg in 1796, and president of the College of William and Mary from 1812 to 1814.

Colorful stories about the rector are never in short supply. As the Reverend Bracken grew older, he became increasingly rotund and fond of the grape. It is said that on his way to conduct a wedding at Yorktown, he may have consumed too much and lost his way, "upset the gigg and broke it," and arrived, wet and muddy, an hour late.

The Chiswell-Bucktrout House, another guest facility, was once owned by Colonel John Chiswell, who became entangled in a 1766 scandal that "put the whole country in a ferment." Charged with killing a man during a tavern brawl, Chiswell was arrested for murder. Friends in high places were able to arrange bail that was unusually low given the circumstances. Chiswell died—probably by his own hand—just before his trial was scheduled to begin.

ABOVE: *The Quarter.*

OPPOSITE ABOVE: *Guests enjoy staying in the snug Chiswell-Bucktrout Kitchen. Toile bed hangings are authentic to the eighteenth century. A period roller map has been placed above the mantel.*

OPPOSITE BELOW: *The Chiswell-Bucktrout Kitchen.*

Colonial Houses once received room service from the Inn by an unusual method designed to be less conspicuous than a van or automobile. As late as the 1970s, a waiter riding a bicycle and balancing a tray was a familiar sight in the Historic Area.

The inviting eighteenth-century Providence Hall House, an original structure, features a master suite, two bed-sitting rooms, board room, garden room and terrace, and tavern-size dining room. The Carriage House contains a parlor suite and bed-sitting room. Providence Hall House is a unique executive retreat and a site for small gatherings. The decoration is that of the Georgian period.

The Providence Hall wings, the first new facilities not connected to the main building of the Inn, are located in a wooded area just to the east. The Executive and Director's wings feature spacious contemporary rooms decorated to harmonize with elements of the Regency style in the Inn. The facility overlooks the tennis courts and two ponds that attract wildlife in season.

*T*he attractive grounds, the woods, the walking trails and jog-ging routes, the lawn bowling and croquet greens, and the mag-nificent fairways and greens of the golf courses all add to the luxuriant atmosphere of the Inn.

Golf blossomed into a fast-growing leisure activity after World War II. Colonial Williamsburg responded by opening a 9-hole course, called the Williamsburg Inn Golf Course, in 1947. Located just south of the Inn, the 2,755-yard layout was designed by Scotsman Fred Findlay. Guests and local players found the course a welcome addition to the other amenities at the Inn.

Len Biles, an Englishman, was the first golf professional. He immediately began to recruit and train local caddies, most of whom, he said, "never saw a course before and never tracked a smothered hook into the deep honeysuckle."

As the popularity of golf continued to increase, Colonial Williamsburg decided to build an 18 hole championship

LEFT: *The seventh hole of the Gold Course overlooks a picturesque, lake-filled valley.*
BELOW: *Hole 18 of the Green Course is a memorable and demanding conclusion to this challenging course.*

course. World-renowned golf course architect Robert Trent Jones, Sr., was selected to design the Golden Horseshoe Golf Course, a 6,700-yard, par 36-35-71 layout that opened for play in 1963.

Robert Trent Jones called the Golden Horseshoe Course "my finest" design. Sensitive to the striking natural beauty of the land, he saved special trees where possible. On many holes, the trees are a hazard that players must consider when they plan their strategy. Jones added flowering and fruiting plant materials to give the course a colorful appearance throughout the seasons.

Carved out of land beyond the south terrace of the Inn, the Golden Horseshoe Course spreads over 125 acres of rolling terrain. A tranquil five-acre lake poses unexpected hazards as the contours of the course meander down ravines and across wooded glens on the way to greens well protected by water and strategically placed bunkers. The Golden Horseshoe is widely known as a challenge, exemplifying Jones's adage that, for an accomplished player, "par should be tough and bogey easy." Most famous—or infamous—is the island hole, the sixteenth, referred to by Jones as "the Gem of the course." This 160-yard par 3 begins with a tee shot that has a dramatic 100-foot vertical drop to a green completely surrounded by water. There is no fairway to salvage wayward shots. The acclaimed sixteenth hole was among the first island greens in this country. It is talked about throughout the golfing world.

The last five holes of the Golden Horseshoe are a golfer's delight and provide a challenging finish to a round. They are the perfect prelude to a different kind of round at the nineteenth hole in the inviting course clubhouse.

The name, "Golden Horseshoe," came from the pages of Virginia's early history. To encourage westward settlement, in 1716 Governor Alexander Spotswood led a company of mounted gentlemen across the Blue Ridge Mountains and into the fertile Shenandoah Valley. The expedition required a great quantity of horseshoes. After returning to Williamsburg, Governor Spotswood gave each of the men a golden horseshoe embedded with valuable stones as a memento of their journey. The governor's companions became known as the Knights of the Golden Horseshoe.

RIGHT: *The serene setting of the Golden Horseshoe Clubhouse attracts golfers and non-golfers alike.*
OVERLEAF: *The par 3 sixteenth hole of the Gold Course, which is well known in the golfing world, offers a breathtaking view of the seventeenth hole unfolding in the background.*

"A great golf course must be a superb blend of shot values, and an artistic flow of lines.

The Golden Horseshoe Golf Course at the Williamsburg Inn is more. The site is a natural arboretum upon which a great golf course has been built.

The over-all result is perfection!"

Robert Trent Jones, Sr., 1963

Rees Jones (left) and Robert Trent Jones, Sr., at Williamsburg, 1992.

Robert Trent Jones, Sr., designed the executive-length Spotswood Course to replace the earlier Williamsburg Inn Golf Course, part of which he incorporated in the Golden Horseshoe. The par-31 Spotswood Course measures 1,865 yards and features different tees on the same nine to create an 18-hole, 3,745 yard, par 62 experience. Along with the challenges of any championship layout, the Spotswood Course compels players to display the mastery of their short game.

When golfers expressed their desire for a second championship golf course, the Foundation asked Rees Jones, son of Robert Trent Jones, to design it. A volley of musket fire signaled the opening of the Golden Horseshoe Green Course. Architect Jones teed off with the first foursome in the tournament that inaugurated the new Green Course in the spring of 1992. The original Golden Horseshoe Course was renamed the Golden Horseshoe Gold Course at the same time.

Jones described the Green Course as "a magnificent piece of land," noting that he had made no attempt to construct a course that would complement or contrast with his father's design of the original Golden Horseshoe. "This was simply a case of the son, 20-some years later, building a course with a little different style. I just tried to build the best course I could."

The Green Course is a links-style golf course reminiscent of those in Scotland. The course has sculptured mounding along the edges of the fairways to help keep errant shots in play. Elaborate bunkering throughout the course is found within the fairway mounds or guarding the greens.

Like the Gold, the Green Course is set among abundant woodlands and dramatic terrain. Water comes into play on six holes. With four different tees from which to select, the Green is an enjoyable test for golfers of every ability. Says Jones, "The great thing about this golf course is that everyone is treated alike."

The Golden Horseshoe golf courses continue to host many tournaments, including the Virginia State Amateur, the Virginia State Senior Amateur, the USGA's Senior Women's Amateur National Championship, and the Mid-Atlantic PGA Section Championships.

Honored over the years with awards and distinctions too numerous to mention, the Golden Horseshoe golf courses have hosted many of the game's greatest players, royalty, and dignitaries from all corners of the world. The

WELCOME . . . JACK NICKLAUS

Golfing great Jack Nicklaus shattered the Golden Horseshoe Golf Course record on September 19, 1967, with a four-under-par 67 performance during an exhibition match sponsored by the Williamsburg Kiwanis Club. Nicklaus was a stroke behind the future U. S. and British Amateur champion Vinnie Giles at the turn and three behind after the tenth hole before he erupted, sinking four birdies and four pars in the final eight holes. His lofty wedge shot for par from a sand bunker on the west side of the eighteenth green clinched the low honors.

Quick to smile, Nicklaus responded to every request for his autograph. When asked why golf was more popular than tennis, he answered, "All tennis courts look the same, and everybody dresses in white."

Rees Jones called the new Green Course "a shotmaker's course. We did not try to make the course tell the player what to do. Instead, we tried to give him several options and allow him to hit different shots."

Williamsburg Inn is proud that so many guests return time and again to revisit the memories and to experience once more the stimulating challenges these picturesque golf courses offer.

Sports-minded guests at the Williamsburg Inn enjoy other outdoor activities as well. Williamsburg's usually mild climate entices tennis enthusiasts to enjoy a set or two on the tennis courts adjacent to the east lawn of the Inn. Eight courts feature clay or hard surfaces on which to exchange serves and volleys.

The oval outdoor swimming pool, a popular favorite among adult guests, was constructed in 1940 on the southwest lawn. Enjoyed as much today as ever before, this pool is fed by spring water that provides a refreshing experience during the warmth of the summer.

ABOVE:
Recreational facilities at the Inn include eight tennis courts.
RIGHT: *One of two refreshing swimming pools at the Inn.*
OPPOSITE ABOVE:
Lawn bowling at the Inn is a popular pastime.
OPPOSITE BELOW:
The lawn bowling practice green.

As the number of guests at the Inn grew, a second pool was added on the west side of the pool house. It has a children's pool alongside to provide enjoyment for the entire family.

The championship lawn bowling green invites guests to participate in this ancient and genteel pastime. Although lawn bowling is a relaxing, easy-paced game, expert players must use strategy and sharply honed skills to win a match on the carefully manicured rink. Members of the Inn's lawn bowling club practice regularly and arrange an occasional tournament with a visiting club. Croquet players can display their deftness with the ball and mallet on the nearby croquet green.

Through the years, guests have frequently commented on how the variety of recreational opportunities at the Inn have enriched and enhanced their stay at Colonial Williamsburg.

*A*mong the interesting things to see and do at Colonial Williamsburg are themed programs—the Antiques Forum in February, Gourmet Weekends in February and March, the Williamsburg Garden Symposium and Garden Week in Virginia in April, Market Days daily during the summer, Publick Times in the fall, and special historical events re-created throughout the year. Seminars in the Historic Area offered through the Williamsburg Institute feature scores of inviting subjects. Weekend programs at the Inn enable guests to acquire new talents or greater expertise in gourmet cooking, wine tasting, floral design, home decorating, and making holiday ornaments.

Each season has much to offer. Many guests like to start a golden fall day with a leisurely breakfast from room service and the morning newspaper beside a blazing fire. When snow falls, Williamsburg becomes a winter wonderland, a photographer's heaven.

Youngsters soon discover a pond filled with immense carp, catfish, and goldfish at the Golden Horseshoe Gold Clubhouse. The pond is also frequented by several dozen mallard ducks and Canada geese. Feeding crusts of bread to the waterfowl is a favorite pastime for adults and children alike.

Wine tasting at the
Williamsburg Inn.

Easter is a special day for the Inn's younger guests who parade in their holiday finery on the terrace. Balloons of all colors mirror the shades of the eggs hidden throughout the grounds. Children delight in discovering the Easter treats.

Young guests who visit the Inn during the summer have their own special menu of fun things to do. They can join the Little Patriot's Club (ages 5-7) or the Capitol Kid's Club (ages 8-12). Croquet, tennis, lawn bowling, hoop rolling, swimming, and story time are favorite activities. Child's-eye tours of Colonial Williamsburg visit the trade shops and the animals. Teenagers sign up for tennis and golf lessons and explore the Historic Area.

OPPOSITE: *Easter excitement.*
ABOVE: *Tennis on one of the Inn's eight courts.*
LEFT: *Everyone enjoys croquet.*

ABOVE: *Tea is a pleasant ritual at the Inn.*
The tiered cake stand holds a tempting
assortment of sweets, finger sandwiches,
and scones and strawberries.
OPPOSITE: *Lady Di roses in the topiary,*
bridal bouquet, and on the cake carry out
the wedding theme. The table is swagged in
white silk that has a laurel wreath design.

OPPOSITE BELOW:

"Beauty" red gerberas, white lisianthus, and silver sage create a striking composition.

OPPOSITE ABOVE:

An anniversary arrangement of "Mont Blanc" white lilies and Aalsmeer gold roses tops a hand-blown glass cylinder.

ABOVE:

The floral designer often conducts educational programs.

BELOW:

"Olivia" pink roses, bells of Ireland, iris, and tulips fill a Delft urn.

*T*he Grand Illumination of the City on the first Sunday in December ushers in the exciting Christmas season. Visitors throng to Williamsburg that weekend to admire the creative decorations, attend the military tattoo, view the fireworks, and stroll the streets amid bonfires and flaming cressets. Glowing candles twinkle in every window in the colonial buildings, a tradition known as "white lighting."

Favorite events in the Historic Area include daily Christmas Decorations Tours, Holiday Balls, the annual display of toys from Christmases past at the Abby Aldrich Rockefeller Folk Art Center, musical presentations, lively feasts and banquets, and theater programs featuring boisterous scenes from popular British comedies presented in early America.

Guests at the Inn participate in special events throughout the holiday season. Festivities begin when guests sing carols as they stroll to the East Lounge to tag the Christmas tree. They are invited to hang a tag with their name and address on the fir. The guest who has traveled the farthest wins a prize. The Yule log ceremony, a traditional Old World custom, is another highlight. After the log is found in the woods behind the Inn, it is brought indoors and burned on Christmas Eve as guests toss holly sprigs on the fire to banish woes in the coming year.

The Regency tree complements the furnishings, architectural details, ambience, and welcoming atmosphere of the lobby at the Williamsburg Inn. The stately tree is trimmed with custom, hand-made ornaments that recall elements of the Regency period. At the top, the striking Prince of Wales crown of needlework and ostrich plumes commemorates one of the great art patrons of that period.

Other favorite activities include demonstrations on how to assemble a traditional gingerbread house and an Old World Yule log by the executive pastry chef, and holiday decorating ideas from the Inn's floral designer. The designer of the immense Regency Christmas tree in the lobby shares the history of the magnificent fir and explains how to make some of the decorations that grace its boughs.

LEFT: *Composed of hand-made gold silk tassels and cording intertwined with poet's laurel, boxwood, and burgundy celosia, the archway swag features gilt cherubs playing musical instruments.*
BELOW: *A gilt angel atop greenery decorates an Ionic column in the lobby.*

Afternoon tea accompanied by special seasonal music programs is a long-standing tradition that occurs every day during the holidays. The Inn places a miniature tree in every guest room, and a special gift arrives on Christmas Day.

The pastry chef demonstrates how to create a Christmas gingerbread scene. Here is his recipe:

◆ Make a cardboard pattern for the house and other elements and use it to cut out the dough.

◆ Mix one pound of powdered sugar and three egg whites together to make a royal icing. Use it to hold the sections together and for decorative icicles.

◆ Cut out all the doors, windows, chimneys, shutters, fencing, animals, trees, and other elements before baking.

◆ After baking, assemble the house and decorate it with candies, nonpareil chocolate disks, or other sweets, including the icing. Arrange the scene and dust with powdered sugar for snow.

LEFT: *The pastry chef creates a Christmas gingerbread scene.*
OPPOSITE: *The inviting East Lounge welcomes Christmas guests.*

For Harold and Anne Kuhn of Wilmore, Kentucky, the Christmas season means it's time to visit the Williamsburg Inn. The Kuhns have spent Christmas at the Inn almost every year since 1967, when the couple decided to spend the holidays in Mrs. Kuhn's home state of Virginia. The visit was an instant success. "We were charmed by everything, including the architecture, the design, the wonderful ambience, and the holiday decorations," Mrs. Kuhn explained.

Don and Mary Ellen Ripley have come from Ohio to spend Christmas at the Inn more than thirty times. Williamsburg is of special interest to them because both were teachers of American history. "The history of the place got us first, then everything began to grow on us," Mr. Ripley pointed out. "We've met some very interesting guests at Christmas. We went to the buildings together, had meals together, and became good friends."

"There are so many wonderful people in the Historic Area and at the Inn—they make us feel at home," Mrs. Ripley said. "We've come to feel more like family than tourists. Williamsburg gives us a family feeling more than other places. That's really what Williamsburg is."

There are more than 300 people on the staff at the Williamsburg Inn.

Every year they . . .

- serve 250,000 meals and 29,494 bottles of wine

- bake 1,397 dozen Christmas cookies

- launder 871,000 pounds of table and bed linens

- arrange more than 100,000 roses

- place 2,343 pounds of chocolates on guests' pillows

Foreword

Few events in the United States have ever commanded more attention, aroused deeper passions, caused wider splits between friends, police and civilians, youth and adults, and even members of the same family, or created havoc on a grander scale among veteran politicians—Republican and Democrat alike—than did the 1968 national conventions for the presidency in Miami Beach and Chicago. Every American has been affected by the results of the two conventions: Miami Beach with its oldtime charades of flag-and-button-encrusted delegates, its rallies, "spontaneous" demonstrations, and its high-pressure, arm-twisting backstage powerplays; Chicago with its White House-ordained candidate, its crusading challengers, anti-war demonstrators, hippies, soft black voices seldom raised in anger, and shouting white voices—profane, outraged, embattled: riot edging toward revolution.

A month before the first convention, while I was in New York seeking an assignment to Viet-Nam for NBC News, Reuven Frank, president of the network, agreed to my Viet-Nam project but then immediately suggested that we attempt a completely unprecedented program series, to appear nightly from the political arenas in Miami Beach and Chicago. I would use still-photographic technique, customarily seen in news magazines, but this time the pictures would be given NBC television transmission, with my own narration as "captions." I would be free to photograph whatever I desired, show whatever pictures I desired, say whatever I desired—for an average of five minutes full network time each convention night. Reuven Frank hoped to give my little "photo-essays of the air" prime time following the Huntley-Brinkley Report, and immediately before the opening gavel. I accepted.

Since my photographs constitute a summation of just one man's view of a series of major news events, there are, naturally, several blank spots in the over-all coverage of what occurred in Miami and Chicago. In Miami Beach, I missed the flare-up of rioting by Negroes across Biscayne Bay in Miami…fighting which claimed several Negro American lives. In appraising the conflict, however, I judged it to be a local skirmish probably unrelated to the activities of the political convention in session a few miles away. As I have stressed in my pictures and text from Miami Beach, Negro Americans played almost no role, either inside or outside Convention Hall, during the Republican National Convention.

In Chicago, I was en route from the stockyards Amphitheater, site of the Democratic National Convention, when the worst confrontation occurred between Senator McCarthy's workers, hippies, newsmen, some bystanders, and the club-swinging, mace-spraying flying wedges of Chicago policemen, in front of the Conrad Hilton Hotel. Thus, I missed the hand-to-hand contact that ensued when the police engaged in what was later described as a "police riot" in the report submitted by Daniel Walker, director of the Chicago Study Team, to the National Commission on the Causes and Prevention of Violence. Nor did I, at any time during my moving around Chicago while the convention was in progress, witness even one of the acts of extreme, obscene provocation—listed in the same "Walker Report"—that have been offered as the causes justifying the Chicago police response. But then—in reflecting upon my own experiences as a photographer of more than twenty-five years of warfare—I also have never photographed at any time, during any fighting and even when there was reason to expect it, hand-to-hand combat on the battlefield, nor have I witnessed it. Neither have I, personally, witnessed atrocities perpetrated by a soldier—the enemy's, or ours. These things happen, but I have never been witness to them. And yet, even with those short-comings, I think that my photographs of war give a fairly clear, and true, but of course subjective idea of what happens when men try to kill one another on ground foreign to them both—often for imprecise reasons.

Similarly, I feel my convention photographs show us as we are—close up: shot during the gathering of our great political clans…our best, worst, most mediocre. Nixon, Rockefeller, Humphrey, McCarthy, hippies, paraders, protesters, professors, Negroes, delegates, dreamers, cops and their killer dogs, wounded Viet-Nam veterans, wounded McCarthyites, wounded spirits along the sidelines…pictures of almost all of us Americans of one breed or another—and forget the politics. I shot my pictures as I found them, rooting for no one, favoring nobody, thrilled with much of what I found, reflective because of new responses discovered within myself and grateful to this experience that released them. I was angry, surely, at some of the situations that exploded into bloodshed, but having been conditioned by a lifetime of reporting violence in its most extreme form on the battlefields of the last quarter century, I believe that I viewed the conflict in Chicago with fairness and in perspective—just as I did the almost country-carnival atmosphere in Miami Beach. Within both conventions one could detect much of the strength and weakness of the political system under which we live today. And during the conventions one could form a rather comprehensive picture of us all…which I have now tried to re-create in book form.

D.D.D.
Easter Sunday
6 April, 1969
Castellaras, France

Self-Portrait: U.S.A.
I Protest!
Yankee Nomad
Picasso's Picassos
The Kremlin
The Private World of Pablo Picasso
This Is War!

One freezing winter morning, thirty years ago in Kansas City,
our family telephone rang. The long-distance operator wanted
David Douglas Duncan. I was connected with a drawling,
cheery-voiced man who casually asked if I'd like to join him
the next day aboard his boat in the Bahama Islands—from which
he was radio-telephoning—prior to leaving for a half year or
so of big-game fishing in the Humboldt Current, off Peru
and Chile. My job? To photograph the activities of an expedition
from the American Museum of Natural History, researching
the habits of broadbill swordfish. But wasn't anybody down
there in the Bahamas worried by the fact that I'd never been
big-game fishing in my life? "You'll learn!" And, of course,
I did—about vastly more than just big-game fishing.

With that single phone call, my life—then jammed to the
gunwales with daydreams, one camera, and inexperience—
changed, quite literally, overnight. Now, I dedicate this book
to the sponsors of that long ago American Museum Expedition,
the two people who gave me a chance to fulfill my daydreams...

HELEN AND MICHAEL LERNER

THE
NATIONAL CONVENTIONS
★ ★ ★
MIAMI BEACH AND CHICAGO

Self-Portrait:
U.S.A.

MIAMI BEACH

Secret Service agent:
laser-beam eyes boring
holes through
everybody with a
single glance...

Presidential aspirant:
fixed campaign grin
masking his
handsome face...

Host governor of the
Miami convention
and Vice-Presidential
aspirant: pouring every
hope into a welcoming
handshake and smile...

Presidential aspirant's
wife: forever smiling
into a wall of faces,
few of them familiar;
and again braced for
the crush of those who
have come to gape,
and others who share a
stake in her husband's
Olympian dream...

Everyone attending a
national convention
has his—or her—
role to play
when a candidate
for President
of these United States
is being chosen.

DAVID DOUGLAS DUNCAN

Self-Portrait: U.S.A.

Harry N. Abrams, Inc.
PUBLISHERS, NEW YORK

Contents

* * *

Traits which brand us Americans—when we mix among other men—
become still more visible when we are seen collectively in places
like Miami Beach, or Chicago—anywhere, I suppose. And yet,
curiously, social and economic forces seem to exert such pressure
upon our two major political parties that their members appear
to be cast in molds so different it is often easy to tell them apart.

Photography & Text: David Douglas Duncan
Design: David Douglas Duncan & Philip Grushkin
Copy Editor: Milton S. Fox: Abrams/New York
Production: David Douglas Duncan & Harry N. Abrams, Inc.
Sheet-fed Gravure: Joh. Enschedé en Zonen/Haarlem/Holland
Bindery: Van Rijmenam/The Hague

My pictures are offered here as a national profile—a big-family photo album—made during
the Republican and Democratic conventions. At that time, for a few hot summer days,
many of the forces that stagnate, rend and torment or embarrass us,
as well as those that give promise of making ours a finer Republic in the future,
were on the surface—festering wounds amid silken complexions—for everyone to see.
It was a great moment for an old war photographer to return home…to aim his cameras at America.

Claude Kirk, governor of Florida, dreamed his dream aloud: he wanted to be Vice-President of the United States, with Nelson Rockefeller in the White House. Kirk had deserted the forces of Richard Nixon early in the year when Rocky declared his candidacy. Now, after greeting the New York governor, Kirk acted as tour conductor en route between airport and Miami Beach, where Rockefeller's first rally was kept waiting.

Rocky wooed Kirk, too, listening eagerly to confidences—or a funny story—that won gales of knee-slapping laughter for Kirk even though the humor of it all seemed lost on the bus driver, Bill Gibbs. Amusing or not, Kirk was of value to Rockefeller, who would need the vote of every delegate when the final count came on the floor, in the ballot race for nomination against one man: Nixon.

With still a mile remaining before arriving at the Miami Beach rally,
Governor Rockefeller leapt to the front stairwell of his special bus
and stood there waving toward the sidewalks of a city
on which almost nobody stood watching—from which no one waved back.

In that moment there was no optimism in the Rockefeller smile—
no victory in his borrowed Churchillian wave.
His fate at Miami Beach was already written in his eyes,
even before the Republican National Convention had begun...
before his own political bandwagon hit town.

Shirt-sleeved candidate shouting himself
hoarse under a searing sun...placards and
banners and balloons and pretty girls
all swearing allegiance to their champion
whose exhortations for greater campaign
efforts and promises of even better times
a-coming get mixed with stern paternal
psychic visions that warn against ignoring
life's many ambushes ahead...bull-horn
corny music...Secret Service agents and
bodyguards up tight back-to-back with
their charge and maybe their candidate...
blazing hot...no protesters...no pickets or
hecklers—no anti-anything...no Negroes—
well, one, probably somebody's chauffeur,
necktie and all; and one kid up a palm
tree. Then the skies opened, the clouds
fell in, everyone ran like hell...it began
to pour. All the time, I suppose, Rocky
knew he didn't have a prayer of getting
more than a sunburn at Miami Beach,
like any tourist barefoot in the sand.

Among all the delegates to the Republican convention, probably no one enjoyed it as fully, tried to pull more hidden wires leading to power, held court to a wider variety of characters—political and otherwise—or got longer mileage out of being the governor of a great state...while projecting himself farther along the victory road to Washington and the White House —the Vice-Presidency, anyway—than did Claude Kirk of Florida...if only in his own bronco-busting, nothing-is-impossible-for-Claude-baby, wide-eyed imagination.

While making a final inspection visit to the cavernous, air-conditioned, TV-wired-and-lighted, radio-plugged, stadium-size but empty Miami Beach Convention Hall, Governor Kirk mounted the speakers podium...where history would start to unfold the next day...and beat everyone to the punch by giving, in full, his acceptance speech as the Republicans' candidate for Vice-President of the United States. Then, turning to me with a semi-sad smile, he said, "It sounds fine, here—better than at home."

Claude Kirk, governor of Florida...
hands raised in victory under the vast
Republican National Convention
emblem...seemed to be listening to the
acclaim of a multitude which only he
could hear. And yet—well-hidden
behind less open faces—in hotel rooms
and bedrooms, and in meeting halls
and secret hideaways throughout the
city and across the land, other
campaigning political hopefuls were
also standing proud and straight, and
with humility, while absorbing
lovingly—in their own imaginations—
every crashing decible in the
mounting explosions of applause that
greeted *their* acceptance speeches.
Rockefeller, Nixon, and all the rest—
like fictitious wonderful Walter Mitty,
intrepid explorer...dauntless pilot...
undefeated prizefighter...Nobel scientist
...super-sleuth...immortal lover...
most decorated of warriors—arrived
in Miami Beach with *their* dream
worlds intact but with their actual
political futures hanging in mid-air
until the Republican tribes assembled,
to count the final ballot.

Claude Kirk was all of *them;* each of *us*.

24

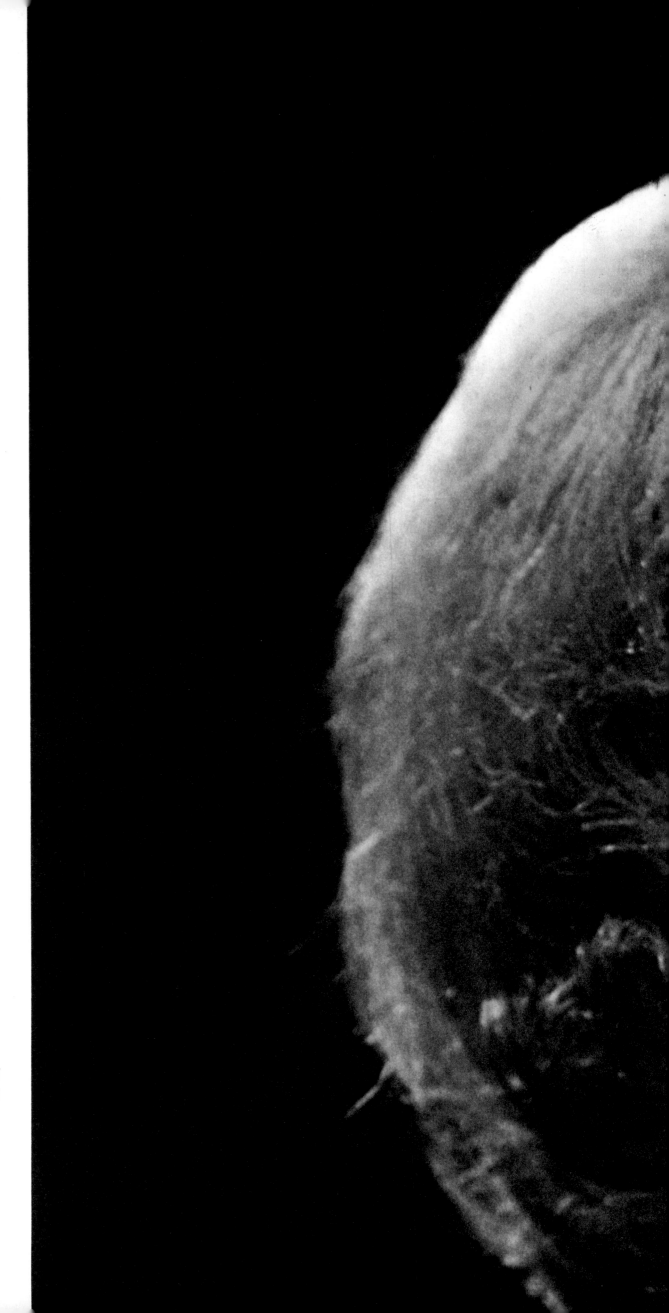

"O say can you see by the dawn's..."

Well—there it goes again!
My friend Metropolitan Opera
bass-baritone George London says
it's almost impossible to sing that song—
he should know...

"as o'er the ramparts we watched..."

he claims he breaks into a cold sweat
just thinking about singing it in front of
an audience...says he'd rather go a
couple of rounds with the world
heavyweight champ himself than belt
out a couple of stanzas as guest vocalist
before the fight begins...

"rockets' red glare and bombs..."

I always figured there was something
wrong with my voice—way back in
Scout camp and at school I had a
terrible time hitting those high notes
but George says even his tenor
friends get hung up when they reach
for the top of some stanzas—then I sort
of shifted gears and knocked off the
lower notes okay...it's funny but even
with her singing it I can't recall the
words just ahead...

"proof through the night that our
flag was still there..."

George says he's championing a cause
to unload The Star-Spangled Banner
for The Battle Hymn of the Republic
which pros and amateurs alike can
really sing and enjoy—but then he
laughs and adds that he'd be run out of
the country on a rail by Southerners
unless somebody rewrites the words
then has a singing Southerner
push it through Congress...

"and the home of the brave."

Not a flaw. Good girl! Maybe George
is exaggerating—anyway it's traditional
to start everything with our anthem and
since it's all we have—that's it!

And it was the same,
every night,
during both of the
national presidential conventions.

Reaching out—through my great telephoto lens—onto the floor
of the Republican convention as the delegates prayed during
the invocation, I found that I was again seeing Americans known
from my childhood years in the Mid-West; plain, dignified,
deeply religious neighbors to be counted on to give help whenever needed, or simply friendship if that was all that one
desired. These were faces I knew. I was comfortable among them.

Secret Service agents stood in each corner of the huge arena, checking by walkie-talkie with other agents posted in lookout eyries far above the convention floor. Swarms of FBI agents, Treasury agents, detectives, policemen in uniform and a great many more in civilian clothes infiltrated the mass of delegates within the hall, or hovered above it on the catwalks. Planeloads of U.S. Marines patrolled ceaselessly in helicopters still farther overhead. It was utterly forbidden for any other aircraft to come within a mile of the arena, and never at less than one thousand feet. The security measures would have seemed excessive, had not America lost a President, a Senator, and its greatest Negro leader, all by assassination—within less than five years.

Where are they?

The question hit
me literally in
the eyes while my
camera swept the
convention floor.

Where—among
those respectable,
good people
whose faces I'd
known since my
childhood days in
Missouri, and
later carried
everywhere as
solid memories
during years spent
working abroad—
where were those
other Americans
of whom I'd read
and heard so
much?
Black...
bearded...
the younger
Americans who
had taken to the
streets as in
Paris and Tokyo,
Rio, Mexico City,
Prague, Panama
—even Shanghai—
with placards and
their gut fury
because of the
total breakdown
of understanding
between so many
levels within
our society today.

Where were *they*
in the placid sea
of gentle, older
Republicans
surrounding me
at the convention
in Miami Beach,
Florida:
U.S.A.?

Thomas E. Dewey, for whom a new word, "gangbuster," was coined in the '30s when he walked away victorious after shooting it out legally against New York's worst: "Murder, Inc.," seemed almost overcome with tears when he was invited to address delegates of the party that knighted him as their giant-killer in '44 to topple a legend—Franklin Delano Roosevelt—Mr. President, himself. In '48, Dewey donned Republican silks once more to race around the campaign circuit against an outrageously blunt, piano-thumping, unpretentious little ex-haberdasher from

Kansas City, who didn't have a chance... Harry S. Truman. Now, again smiling down from the podium, looking for all the world like their new Presidential candidate and as though twenty in-between years simply had not existed, as though they never even touched him or that voice, Thomas Dewey filled Convention Hall with a music rare, today—the deep flowing cadences of our English language being spoken beautifully, with affection. And the magic of his voice fell as a caress upon many among the delegates, for whom, suddenly, twenty years had miraculously vanished—too.

White-plumed Everett Dirksen, imperious to a degree seldom seen today,
stood cold and aloof—the Old Bird himself on the topmost crag—
awaiting silence...*demanding* silence...from all of the convention
delegates before he would share a single line of the Republican
Party's newly-hatched Platform. The Senator from Illinois seemed
haughty and secure in his role as party oracle, and equally sure of the
image he created; of being the original American Bald Eagle, who now
had plummeted down to guard the sacred Platform, and therein every
citizen's destiny, before soaring away again to his customary lair—
inside the Great Seal of the United States.

"There will be silence!" The rumble of delegates' voices still
roiled the air waves churning up around Senator Dirksen's ears.
"There...will...be...SILENCE!" The air waves cleared a little, but
then static arose from the shifting of over twenty-five hundred chairs.
"T-H-E-R-E...W-I-L-L...B-E...S-I-L-E-N-C-E!" And there was.
"If there is NOT silence you will NOT hear this Platform.
If there IS silence, you shall hear this Platform—a majestic document—
the most succinctly you will ever hear it—because when there IS silence...
I shall read it."

The muscle-jawed young range rider from Wyoming turned slowly in his
metal-and-plastic convention saddle, squinted up into the haze of rostrum
spotlights—and listened, along with most of the other delegates.

Listening to a reading of the Platform was not easy, despite Senator Dirksen's stentorian skill. Perhaps no political party's proclamation could ever hold an audience of thousands for more than a few minutes—especially when they are being slow-baked under television spotlights and harassed by the possibility that a camera's probing eye might reveal them in unguarded, coke-drinking, sandwich-snacking, or lids-closed reflective moments…unmindful of their responsibilities to those good folks back home, slouched comfortably in dark privacy before TV screens. But there were a few delegates who had been attending conventions since before television's birth, in the era when reporting by radio was considered sensational—Old Timers, who now yawned and dozed away, comfortable in the dignity and insulation of their years.

For a mad moment it seemed I was covering the wrong story—
that I'd targeted-in on the wrong clusters of night-lights
blasting holes through Miami's tourist-and-fun-beckoning sky.

In my viewfinder, I'd found some Damon Runyon characters
playing a *Form*—and wondered about picking up a hot tip—then
looked closer: it read *Republican Platform*, not *Racing Form*.

He simply stood there—a mountain of a man around whose flag-crowned, straw-hat summit the everyday life of his delegation parted and swirled and then regrouped, but left him unmoved. Applauding to himself…whistling to himself…reflecting to himself—he appeared to be one of the loneliest of all humans on this teeming earth. And yet, he was contributing to the group effort of the convention. He was The Delegate. His vote was equal to any other in the land, and the most important single cog in the whole complex machine which is our form of government. Somewhere behind the nearly inscrutable choice of The Delegate, and the *always* secret choice of the voter, our Presidency survives.

Two hundred million Americans; counting us all.
Twenty million—ten percent—Negro Americans.
Twenty-six hundred sixty-two delegates and alternates
at this Republican National Convention; counting all.
Eighty-two Negro Republicans—about three percent—
sprinkled somewhere out on that convention floor.
Dream for all ... Mr. Genoa S. Washington, of Chicago.

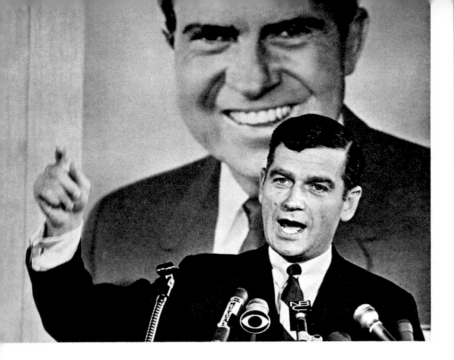

Oregon's Senator Mark Hatfield sparkled for TV,
at one of the Nixon camp's mid-morning
press conferences, but gave no hint other than
a display of campaign-poster smiles that
his own Walter Mitty dream-balloon, stamped
HATFIELD FOR VICE-PRESIDENT,
had been seen over Miami by "The Boss," himself.

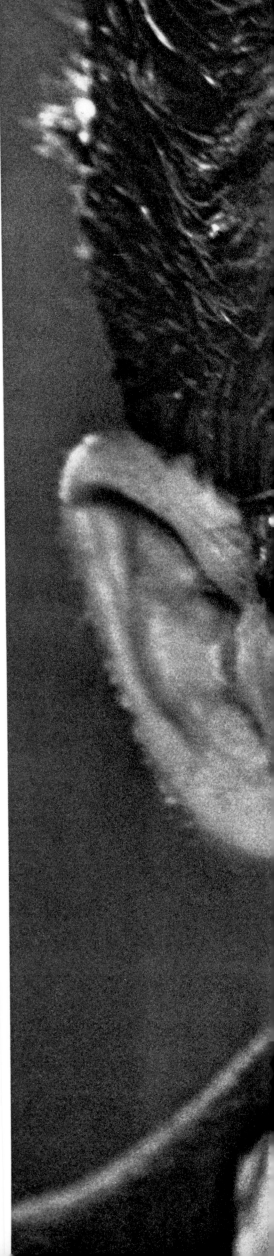

Mr. Law 'n' Order...Sam Thunderbolt, Sheriff of Tombstone...Tricky Dick, Scourge of Commies—Liberals—Democrats...Richard the Chicken-Hearted, fearing The Debate on TV...all of these name tags, and more; also Vice-President of the United States for eight years under General of the Armies, Dwight David Eisenhower; and my friend since that day twenty-five years ago in the Solomon Islands, where he was a scrawny Navy lieutenant who resupplied this scrawnier Marine lieutenant with gear, when I re-entered the Allied perimeter after fighting with a battle group of Fijian guerrillas behind the Japanese line on Bougainville. Now, he stood before a battalion of us correspondents assembled for his first Miami Beach press conference. I watched him field one question after another with calm, almost sledge-hammer assurance, but wary, too, of that sleeper-question that would trip him— to splash devastating headlines across the country, and on around the world.

And I thought back—as I kept my super-telephoto lens on that rough, ever-changing, not handsome but strangely photogenic face—to how often we had assured one another it was time that we shoot a story together: in '53, when he made his first trip abroad as Vice-President; in '56, when he came to Vienna to tour the Austro-Hungarian border during the Budapest Revolution; then, again, in '59, when he word-duelled with Nikita Khrushchev in that Moscow Trade Fair kitchen; and other times now forgotten. But I never photographed him, not once.

Today, Richard Milhous Nixon, you're in my viewfinder...let's see you escape!

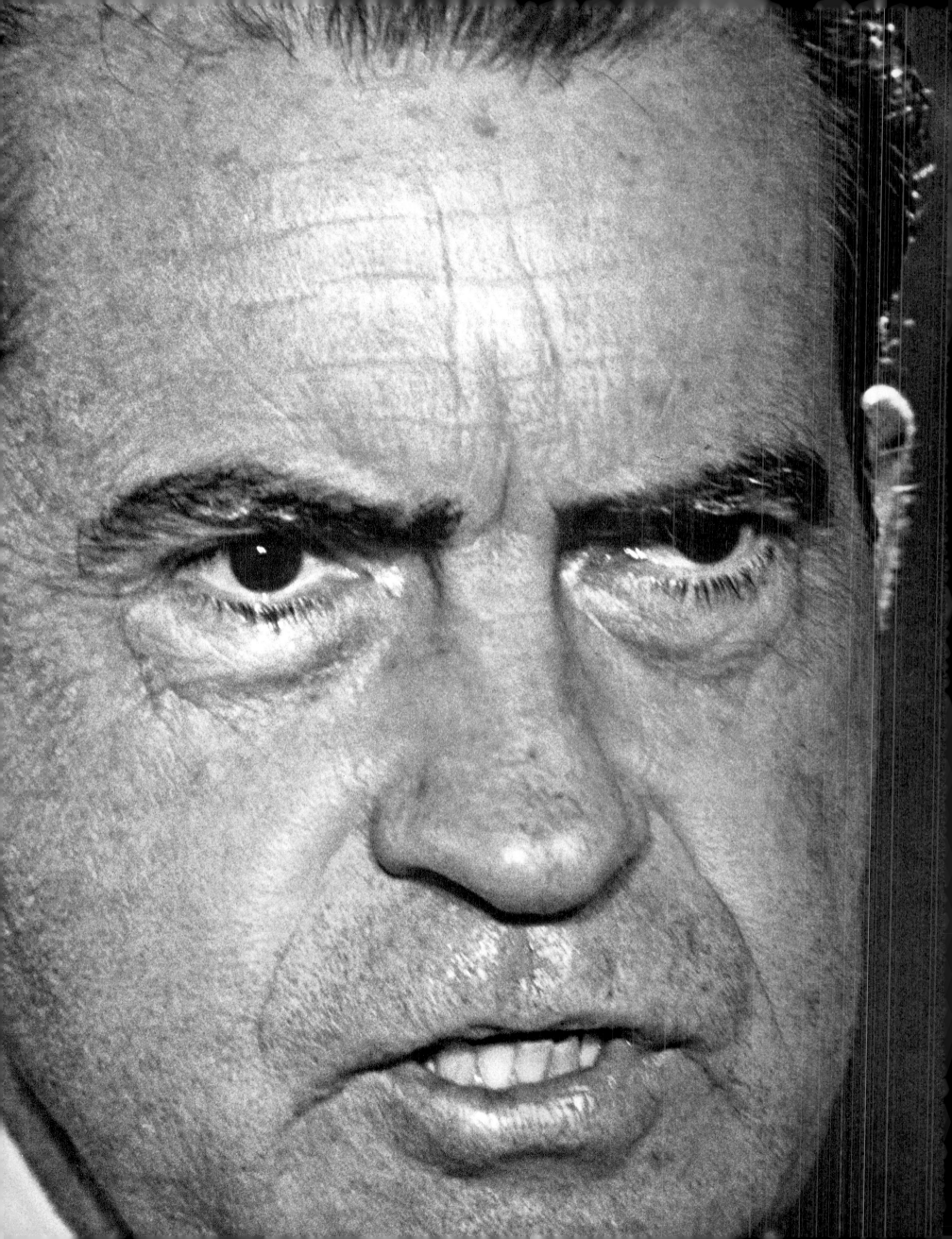

He had an easy time with the questions from the correspondents at his right in that first press conference; in fact, he seemed almost relaxed, to be coasting through a situation which several years earlier, in California, had battered him to his knees. But, of course, at that time he had just lost the election for governor. Today, much tougher and most probably wiser, he still seemed cautious yet sure-footed in finding his way through the minefield of questions, planted there by professionals—few of them his friends. He also replied with laughter: something new.

A far more dangerous barrage of questions pounded Nixon from correspondents at his left: "What will you do, if President, about curtailing crime in our streets; preventing race riots in our ghettoes; giving promise of a less materialistic future to our youth; bringing peace with honor—as you earlier stated you can—in Viet-Nam?" On all points except Viet-Nam (which he said he refused to discuss while the Paris peace talks were in progress, or until he was President) his replies were sufficient to be news, but I wondered about the deeper answers he kept to himself.

While focusing on Nixon's hands and face, I tried to imagine what the politician's world was like before radio, jet plane—or today's televized press conference: image-maker; sounding board; semi-official diplomatic channel; vanity showcase; political weapon with deadly radiation fallout. And as I followed his hands—those of a concert master—I kept thinking how careful Big Brass must be with TV cameras, knowing an earth satellite is behind them to relay instantly *this* careless gesture...*this* angry scowl...*this* tired body, onto screens God-knows-where: where these tired *words* might be misunderstood, too. I wondered how anyone, seeing the sadly ravaged faces of men who became President, could ever want that job.

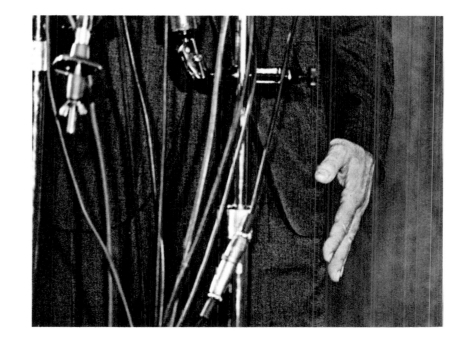

Luck was with me at Miami Beach. When Richard Nixon finished his
first press conference in his headquarters hotel, I caught his eye through
echelons of other photographers, correspondents, TV reporters, and
hordes of NIXON'S THE ONE button-emblazoned characters—each of
them pressing forward with appeals for special consideration of his
"greatest-idea-in-the-world" news story…just as I was, too.
But my twenty-five year head start was unbeatable. Dick Nixon remembered.
He answered my five-second presentation with an index finger jabbed
at an aide already headed for their top-floor command post:
"He'll phone you within one hour."

The next night—during the nominations—I was to be the
only photographer or correspondent permitted past the staff floors of
Nixon's GHQ; past those NIXON'S THE ONE mural-size posters that
looked only vaguely like the man I'd watched through my telephoto;
past the special Wackenhut security officers at every door;
and all the way up to the command penthouse itself, of "The Boss."

Richard Nixon, soon to be
accepted, again, or rejected,
as Republican nominee for
President, stood framed in
the bright rectangle of his
GHQ penthouse doorway,
beyond Secret Service agent
and aide—far, indeed, from
the wartime mangrove swamp
where he scrounged a pair of
almost-new boots to replace
those that I'd just ruined.

Nixon's command post at the Republican convention
was a converted penthouse of his hotel; transformed
only by the addition of portable television sets in
all rooms, and extra telephones tied to a labyrinthine
communications and operations complex cramming the
floors just below him. Above him, in a rooftop sauna,
there was a blackboard-lined, Pentagon-size chart room
for plotting every signal—no matter how feeble—
indicating all activity across the city and nation,
of both his supporters and his opponents, during the
critical minutes leading up to the nomination and
final ballot. Also on the rooftop, an around-the-clock,
Nixon-staffed duplicate telephone switchboard was
operating independent of that in the hotel. Finally,
hidden in a tiny, photograph-filled room, still another
communications network was manned by agents of
the Secret Service, whose somber-eyed colleagues in the
hotel below screened every face entering the candidate's
realm. Outside was another world: tourist-filled Miami.

No pressure was reflected in the face of Nixon as he
sat listening—scarcely speaking—to the men who were
some of his closest aides...Ziegler, Haldeman, Chapin,
Klein...while they voiced opinions on final trends in
the conventionwide balloting picture. One report hurt:
he reacted like an old general—ready to attack again.
Then they all left the room, and he was alone.

Just before his aides left the room, Nixon had pointed with his pen to the large yellow lawyer's notebook on his knee—and looked carefully into each face: "There will be no—NO—copies of this speech released to the press or TV before I give it myself. It's a speech for listening, not reading, and I don't want any reporter or commentator beating me to my own lines until I give them myself. Am I clear? No copies to anybody! Besides, it's a pretty good speech. At least, I think so...sort of like poetry."

When the others were gone, Nixon took his notebook into an alcoved window niche overlooking the night-darkened sands of Miami Beach and began to write in a full, clear hand, words I could not help but read in my viewfinder: "My fellow Americans, the long night for America is about to end. The time has come for us to leave the valley of despair and climb the mountain so that..."

Holy smoke—the guy is revamping his acceptance speech
right under my lens...like I'm not even here...
as though I'm not a reporter, with a TV show of my own!

Richard Nixon was still probing for weak lines in his speech, when word came that his name was being placed in nomination by the governor of Maryland, Spiro Agnew. Aides refilled the room to take seats arcing away from "The Boss"—who sat in an easy chair watching and listening to Governor Agnew. There was no other voice in the room. At the precise moment he was nominated, Dick Nixon shifted his gaze from the television screen, to me, and said: "Dave, do you remember those *tall* bottles of Australian beer we had on Bougainville? Oh, that's right, you only liked orange juice—but for the rest of us they were just great!" Then, the voice of Governor Agnew again filled the room.

Richard Nixon
seeing himself
nominated for
President
was not to be
mistaken for
another man of
average dreams.

The moment Governor Agnew's
speech had ended, Convention Hall
erupted with brass bands, bursting
balloons and bouncing banners,
dangling ribbons, flags, state seals,
flowers, and ikon-like posters
of a new Republican saviour,
Richard Nixon...who was
watching the traditional spectacle
and sinking ever lower into his easy
chair; finally covering his eyes with
his hand as though to blot out the
whole nationwide telecast farce—
which seemed a cross hard to bear.

After twelve minutes—of the maximum twenty allotted each nominee by convention rules—Nixon reared back in his chair, looked up at an aide, and exploded: "This is baloney! It's a waste of time. It should never last more than ten minutes—ever!" Then, with a glance at me, he added, "Come on, Dave. Let's get some fresh air." And he was out of that penthouse, into a private elevator—flanked by Secret Service agents—and down in the basement of his hotel, into the backseat of a low-slung, Secret Service-driven limousine that careened away into the soft Florida night...all in the time it took the demonstrators back at Convention Hall to bang out a couple of more ear-killers on their big drums and pop a few of their balloons.

Luck befriended me again, after Dick Nixon returned from his half-hour midnight drive up the beach. Back at the penthouse doorway, he explained I'd have to stop shooting pictures of him until after the balloting, since that story had been given to another TV network. Then, saying he still had something "special" for me in a few hours: "Don't leave the hotel!" he vanished behind his command post door.

At that moment, the door of the *opposite* penthouse swung open to reveal Tricia Nixon; her escort, Ed Cox; David Eisenhower and his fiancée, Julie Nixon; all watching the first-ballot roll call, down at Convention Hall.

Double-hamburgers, milk, and Tricia Nixon—remote, silent, daydreaming... seemingly lost in a cloud-world of her own: another Alice in Wonderland. Maybe—but with a well-developed political computer behind her soft dark-blue eyes, which rarely turned away from the TV screen where her father was beating off attacks by Rockefeller, Reagan—and perennial loner, Harold Stassen—who were trying to kill Nixon's drive to first-ballot victory. Tricia saw her Dad winning... but in what cloud-world were Julie and David?

*Who thinks about conventions—or ballots—or anything, really,
except ourselves...when in love.*

My "special" phone call came from Nixon's headquarters
shortly after he won the nomination: "Be back at the
penthouse before 2 o'clock—A.M.! The Boss said to tell
you he has a final exclusive picture for you tonight."
On arriving outside Nixon's door, I found the Reverend
Billy Graham—seated. Having never seen him, my mental
image was so strong of a-man-in-his-pulpit that I almost
missed him...like missing Gandhi in a tuxedo. Tom Dewey
hurried into the penthouse. Nixon arrived. He escorted
the Reverend Graham inside, then looked back—
with the slightest wink—and left the door open, for me.

I walked into
a pre-dawn,
super-secret
pow-wow of
Republican
medicine men
from across
the nation,
seated in a
great circle
before their
new chief.
They must have
already smoked
the peace pipe.
Dead center,
just in front
of me, I saw
Goldwater—
Fannin—
Dewey—
Thurmond:
and on around
the teepee,
Mundt, Finch,
Fong, Brownell;
two Rhodeses;
Mitchell;
Knowland, of
the California
Reagan tribe;
Hall, of the
New York tribe
of Rockefeller;
and Reverend
Billy Graham.
They had been
called together
to accept as
their chief's
running mate
an untested
tribal warrior,
Spiro Agnew,
of Maryland...
who had just
stood before
their entire
council to
nominate—
Chief Richard
Milhous
Nixon
for
President
of the
United States.

That last night of the convention was *the* night at Convention Hall for the new Republican candidate.

"Eight years ago, I had the highest honor of accepting your nomination for President of the United States. Tonight, I again proudly accept that nomination...

"We make history tonight—not for ourselves but for the ages. The choice we make in 1968 will determine not only the future of America but the future of peace and freedom in the world for the last third of the Twentieth Century. And the question that we answer tonight: can America meet this great challenge?..."

Hey, amigo, where's the "mountain" I saw in your speech?

"...as we look at America, we see cities enveloped in smoke and flame. We hear sirens in the night. We see Americans dying on distant battlefields abroad. We see Americans hating each other; fighting each other; killing each other at home. And as we see and hear these things, millions of Americans cry out in anguish. Did we come all this way for this? Did American boys die in Normandy...Korea...Valley Forge for this?..."

Surely, there is no place, here, for a mountain!

"Listen to the answer to those questions. It is another voice. It is the quiet voice in the tumult and the shouting. It is the voice of the great majority of Americans, the forgotten Americans—the non-shouters; the non-demonstrators. They are not racists or sick; they are not guilty of the crime that plagues the land. They are black and they are white—they're native born and foreign born—they're young and they're old. They work in American factories. They run America's businesses. They serve in government. They provide most of the soldiers who died to keep us free. They give drive to the spirit of America. They give lift to the American Dream. They give steel to the backbone of America. They are good people, they are decent people; they work, and they save, and they pay their taxes, and they care...This I say to you tonight is the real voice of America..."

*Great, but where...*suddenly, I heard words I'd read!

"...the long dark night for America is about to end. The time has come for us to leave the valley of despair and climb the mountain so that we may see the glory of the dawn—a new day for America, and a new dawn for peace and freedom in the world."

The last paragraph! And then he stood there, bathed in applause...television spotlights...and the satisfaction of having made this first enormous step, within his own Walter Mitty dream, come true.

Eyes closed, he seemed lost amongst the echoes of his own words:
"Tonight, I see the face of a child...he's an American child...
he dreams the dreams of a child...yet he awakens to a living
nightmare of poverty, neglect and despair...to millions of children
of this rich land, this is their prospect of the future. But...
I see another child tonight...he dreams of far away places...it
seems like an impossible dream. But he is helped on his journey
...a father who had to go to work before he finished the sixth grade
...a gentle, Quaker mother...a courageous wife and loyal
children stood by him in victory and also defeat...And tonight he
stands before you—nominated for President of the United States.
You can see why I believe so deeply in the American Dream."

Then Billy Graham prayed for us all...

...and Convention Hall
was tidied up for the Flower Show.

THE
NATIONAL CONVENTIONS
★ ★ ★
CHICAGO AND MIAMI BEACH

Self-Portrait:
U. S. A.

CHICAGO

Chicago…of a summer evening:

"No to LBJ"

"A breath of fresh air
Gene McCarthy"

"Humphrey"

"A breath of fresh…
Gene McCarthy"

"HHH
Let a Winner
Lead the Way"

"A breath of…
Gene Mc…"

"HHH
Young Citizens
for Humphrey"

"A breath…
Gene…"

"We Love You Hubert"

And, "Equal Represent-…"
on the rear perimeter of the
Conrad Hilton Hotel lobby,
supposedly neutral ground—
discothèque DMZ of Chicago's
Democratic National Convention.

Another battle of ink pots!

Apparently I was in the front
trenches of a typical teen-agers'
political-poster war: all fun.
One faction, obviously, had the
stronger psycho-warfare team.
But, as a Marine private
dryly observed at *the* DMZ,
after coming straight from
California boot-camp—and
as I sensed upon arrival in
Chicago from my Miami Beach
political boot-camp training,
amid the middle-aged languor
of the Republican Convention—
*"This place is going to be
Something Else!"*

Some talk change
Others cause it.

hrey

The teen-agers all had their champions…
Hubert Horatio Humphrey:
Vice-President of the United States;
blessed by the abdicating President
as the White House favorite for the nomination—
but was that chain-mail touch really a blessing?
Eugene McCarthy:
Senator from Minnesota;
self-sanctified, one-sermon, low-key crusader who
seemed as astounded as anyone when, while tilting with
spectres in New Hampshire, he unhorsed the Old King himself—
but was that sufficient reason to make him heir to the throne?

In addition to politically awakened teen-agers, Chicago was host to visitors who walked the convention city championing causes special to themselves. Their main beat was Michigan Avenue in front of the Conrad Hilton Hotel, GHQ for both Humphrey and McCarthy, besides being home base for many journalists and television units covering nomination week.

Some placards were grimly dogmatic. Other posters carried messages so verbose as to be unreadable in the few moments available when passing them in the street; perhaps a shame because of the obvious care lavished upon their preparation.

Then, there were the Untouchables—hippies—rolled up in their blankets in the city's parks; or ostentatiously, openly, practicing professionally lamentable guerrilla tactics on the same trampled grass, but only for TV cameras and even then only in platoon strength. Yet possibly those unkempt, bearded ones were yippies—no need for any concern about such gorillas. Other beards were festooned Spanish moss-style from heroic monuments. And everyday exhibitionist hippies lay sprawled before the Art Institute seeking hidden meanings in each other's traumas, which made access difficult to treasures in the building behind their unwashed backs.

When not plagued with hippie invasions,
or the threat of ghetto-gang uprisings,
one of the great questions nagging Chicagoans
—convention week or any other time—
is the riddle of Picasso's towering, 160-ton
sculpture which dominates the Civic Center forum.

Hey—fella—just what is it?
What does it mean…if anything?

The artist told Chicago architect William Hartmann,
who brought the colossus to his city, that it is a woman.
One afternoon in his studio, the same Pablo Picasso
told me it is a portrait of his great Afghan hound, Kabul.
None of which is important.
What really matters in Chicago's Civic Center forum,
and out across the rest of our troubled country,
is how we Americans are going to view each other in the future,
and how we will share our dreams.

Is Picasso's
sculpture a
long-nosed,
silken-eared
Afghan hound
named Kabul,
or a woman—
a classic-
profiled,
semi-veiled
Spanish nun?

*Hey, fella!
Take your
pick…*

The answer,
of course,
is that it
is both.
How great
we would be
if we viewed
life itself
as easily
from
both sides—
and then
accepted it.

109

Very few
out-of-town
delegates to the
Chicago convention
found time to see
any of the great
paintings filling
the Art Institute
to its ceilings;
pictures known
to local delegates
since earliest
childhood, despite
their reputation
for karate-style,
big-boss politics—
now rumored to be
threatening those
Democrats warily
gathering outside.

A little boy, exhausted from following his parents during their tour of Chicago Art Institute masterworks, stretched out at full length to gaze around the walls dominated by a painting of Jesus in manacles before Pontius Pilate's legionnaires: Edouard Manet's monumental canvas, *The Mocking of Christ*. That hushed gallery seemed far more distant than a few miles from the stockyards and the shoe-shine stand of two boys whose favorite school-vacation customers were the casual, combat-helmeted, bull-shouldered legionnaires of the grim Prelate of Chicago—Mayor Richard J. Daley. He had ordered every available policeman to line duty as precaution against rumored black-ghetto rebellions, the terrorism promised by infiltrating yippies, and the danger of assassination attempts upon the lives of his fellow Democratic delegates arriving at the Amphitheater, one street from the boys' shoe-shine stand. Mayor Daley—reportedly warned by the FBI—was prepared. In addition to his city forces, he had requested and received a promise of support from the specially-mobilized Illinois National Guard—troopers on 24-hour-a-day standby alert— now ready to move upon the city with armor, if needed. A total of 22,000 armed men (more than a U.S. Army division) stood poised to subdue other Americans in Chicago's streets.

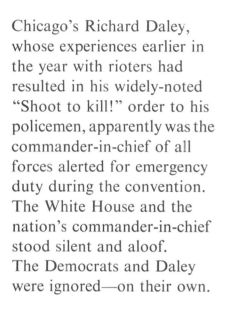

Chicago's Richard Daley, whose experiences earlier in the year with rioters had resulted in his widely-noted "Shoot to kill!" order to his policemen, apparently was the commander-in-chief of all forces alerted for emergency duty during the convention. The White House and the nation's commander-in-chief stood silent and aloof. The Democrats and Daley were ignored—on their own.

Probably few convention delegates
arrived in Chicago harboring the assumption
they were meeting on neutral ground to nominate
their candidate for President. Still, it must
have been embarrassing—even irritating—
for the Democrats to find they had entered
"Daley Country," U.S.A., as though Chicago
were a separate realm within the Union;
which, in some ways, it was!

The delegates were perhaps most unnerved—
after seeing Big Brother's name splashed everywhere—
to find his unblinking, plastic eyes waiting
even under their hotel-room telephones.
In all of Chicago there was no escape.
Mayor Daley's fief, during nomination week,
began to seem as unreal to some Americans as was that earlier,
Republican, political-circus masquerade in Miami Beach.

Mayor Daley was a genial, compulsive conventioneer…
friend of unions—but not of striking cab drivers…
friend of most ethnic groups—but not of ghetto Negroes…
friend of local ward-heelers; the governor;
the Vice-President; the President…
the convention came to Chicago.

At first glance, delegates to the national convention might have assumed they were being remiss in their obligations to "the people" if they did not heed those signs plastered upon the walls and windows of Chicago shouting DALEY, among others blaring WELCOME and HELLO DEMOCRATS!

By a curious coincidence, every poster in the city revealed a common, boring style: their design and choice of type face were identical. But that didn't appear to distress their subject nearly as much as did the handiwork of one Cook County artist, who had difficulty interpreting his patron's latest dream.

Humble…self-effacing…devout family man…
dedicated civic servant…enormously efficient…
astute economist…brilliant political tactician…
clever administrator—also, really warm and friendly—
so, why *not* promote DALEY FOR PRESIDENT among the
WELCOME placards? Besides, nobody would ever guess
shy Mayor Daley ordered all of those posters, himself.
Anyway—WELCOME—welcome, brother delegates…
welcome to the Chicago stockyards Amphitheater and a
"wide open" Democratic National Convention.

WELCOME DEMOCRATS

MAYOR
RICHARD J.
DALEY

DALEY FOR PRESIDENT

HELLO!

WELCOME…

Yes sir…
Hello delegates!

But what about t-h-e-m?

Oh, those canine-cops
with their 500-pounds-
per-square-inch-a-bite-
killers that patrol the
Amphitheater perimeter,
starting at dusk?
Yeah—them! Oh, they
won't attack if your
press pass is in order.

And if they can't read?

Well then, fella, I'd
guess they'll pop your
leg like a chicken bone.

225

Even before the Democratic National Convention was
gavelled into its first day's session, an historic fight
had begun on an unlikely battlefield—the floor of
the International Ballroom, in the Conrad Hilton Hotel.

For five pre-convention days, brash newcomers among
the party's southern ranks—mostly Negroes—fought
for seats with their states' delegations, and recognition
by the omnipotent Convention Credentials Committee.

The Credentials Committee exercised absolute control over the
seating of all delegates to Chicago. Thus, on the witness stand,
before a tribunal in which every state was represented, America's
racial issue was seen in microcosm: our innocence...our blatant
acceptance of traditional inequities...our frontier puritanism and
outrage toward injustice...our intolerance of another's fears...
our efforts to weave a more durable national fabric in which
to shield everyone—tomorrow. And our impatience with it all!

The Reverend-witness from Georgia stood choked on words
he had saved for a lifetime; simple words, explaining why he had
come to Chicago to appear for these few moments before other
Democrats from all the land: they surely could not *know*
that children, like his, were beaten simply for going to school,
and homes, like his, were bombed and burned at night only because
he lived there; that...but it was a tattered old tale of misery.
His plea to seat protesting men in Georgia's delegation, when they
nominated a candidate for President, fell upon some nearly deaf ears
in the Credentials Committee—apparently, just like in Georgia.

The Georgia minister—with his friend and counsellor at his shoulder—tried to span with words the distance between his life and that enjoyed by most of the Credentials Committeemen. It was a journey through terrain familiar to a few delegates—they knew every landmark along the way.

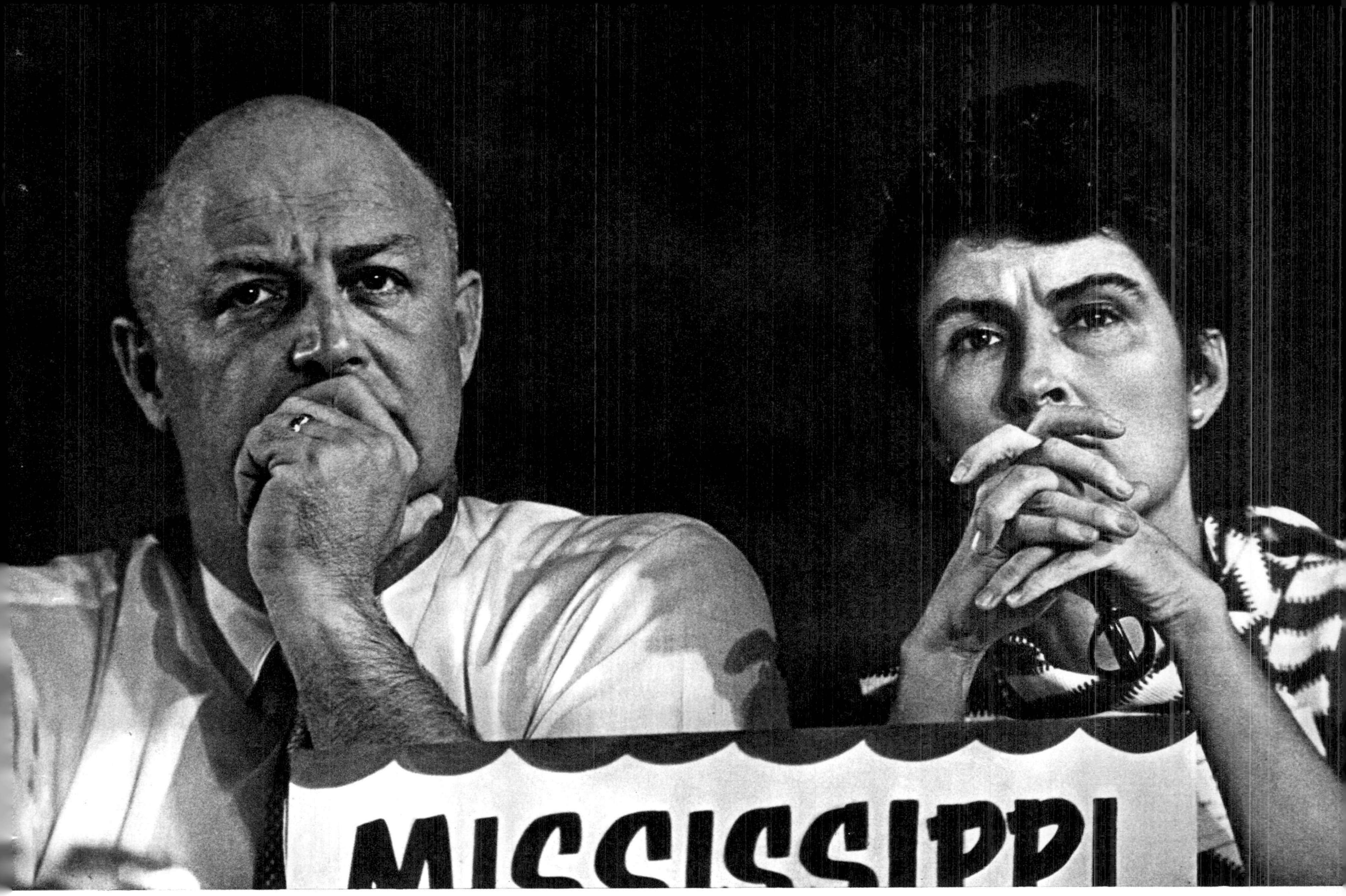

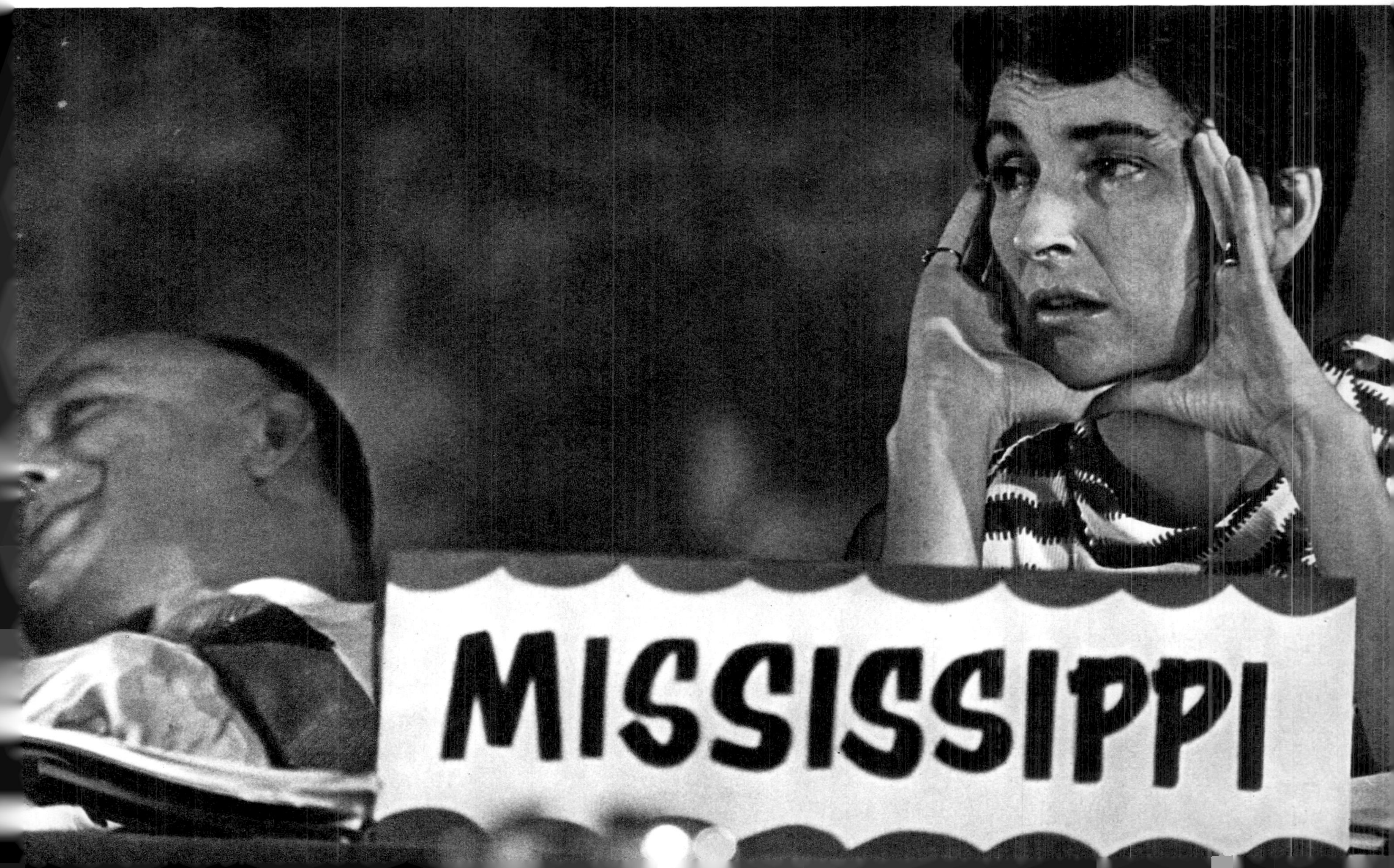
MISSISSIPPI

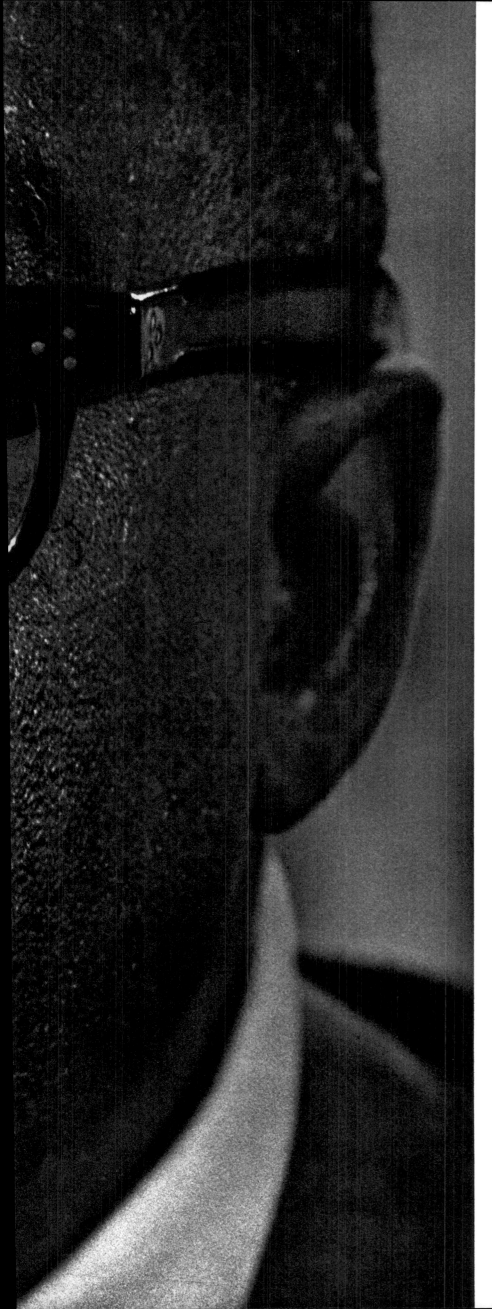

As the Reverend-witness from Americus, Georgia, testified before the Credentials Committee, a pensive, stockily-built, slow-smoking delegate from Connecticut sat listening—his eyes searching the face of the southerner. In the moment before the visitor turned to leave the witness stand, the Connecticut delegate reached for a nearby microphone—to ask one question: "Pardon me, Reverend. But I was born in Americus. Do you think, if I were to return there, today, I might be sent back here to Chicago as a delegate to this convention?" The minister's whispered reply, "Most unlikely!" was nearly lost as laughter swept one section of the Credentials Committee, then rolled farther out, to engulf the International Ballroom.

MISSISSIPPI

The minister
from Americus
left the stand,
and Chairman
Richard. J. Hughes,
the governor of
New Jersey, called
for another witness.
The hearing
of all challengers
then continued.

Before still another witness stepped up to challenge the party's Credentials Committee on the structure of membership of his state's delegation to the convention, an indignant, articulate lawyer with the shoulders of a professional wrestler took the stand. With cropped head rammed forward and his eyes fixed upon Chairman Richard Hughes, the new witness stated that he was a representative of the governor of Georgia, and that he regretted the distortions being aired before the Credentials Committee; distortions maligning the honor both of Georgia and her governor, who now was finally permitting his name to be placed before the nation itself, as another candidate for President of the United States. The lawyer-witness neglected to mention the fact that the presidential aspirant from Georgia had run for governor as a righteous segregationist, who reportedly gave voters ax handles in his restaurant against "sit-in" strikers—as evidence of the purity of his convictions.

The following challenger stood alone; a tall, slender, young legislator—from Atlanta—who bent low over the microphone, looked out into the faces of the tribunal, and said:
"My name...is Julian Bond."
He told of his life as a Georgia Negro; of his hopes for the black citizens of our country; of their dreams. And as he spoke a hush fell upon that room—where all America listened.

137

Connecticut

Alabama

Alabama

Louisiana

Arkansas

Mississippi

Maryland

Alaska

There was no sound in the room…not a voice…no creaking chair.
Only silence…Julian Bond had finished.
Far away in the audience, the lips of an impassioned orator
opened…but they were silent, too.

Where have I seen these faces before? Yes…I remember…
it was Palestine immediately after World War II…these were the
eyes of the Old Jews who had come home from the ashes of Europe,
and the ashes of two thousand years of dreams before them…but where,
where if not here, is the Jerusalem of our Old Negroes?

Then the next witness—from Louisiana—took the stand.

FURMAN TEMPLET

Idealism—perhaps America's most resilient national trait—was the origin, probably
the foundation, of the gentle appeal made by Senator George McGovern when,
at the last possible moment, he packed up his South Dakota family and hit the
presidential campaign trail for Chicago and the Democratic National Convention.

Along the road, meeting improvised schedules, Senator McGovern's first, crusading,
warning-of-disaster speeches were sparsely attended, though his audiences were plainly
concerned and respectful. Then, abruptly, the Senator's platform style changed.
His speech punchlines grew sharper. His anti-Viet-Nam war and anti-administration
broadsides were fired in volleys that detonated with greater impact. He was news!

Senator McGovern's meager staff had been bolstered by the arrival of a heavyweight
professional, one of the most experienced press advisers in the land: Pierre Salinger.
Formerly press secretary of President John Kennedy; then, more recently, a press
consultant to his brother, Senator Robert Kennedy, Pierre Salinger was now starting
out again—but, certainly, with an inner sense of irreplaceable loss, and bitter nostalgia.

153

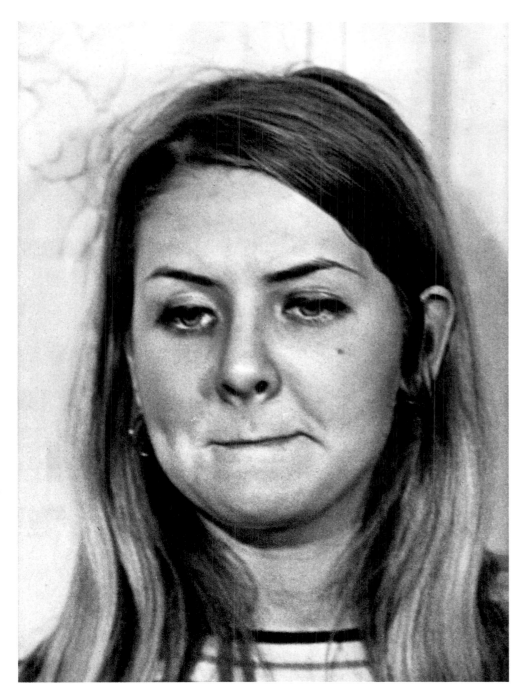

Senator George McGovern—flanked by his wife and his daughters, and
his closest aides—was catapulted straight into his first Chicago
press conference within minutes after his campaign plane touched
down from California. It was a typical—ideal—election-time scene:
the clean-cut, athletic, level-eyed, forthright, fact-filled candidate;
the stunning, adoringly attentive wife at his side; their handsome
family just behind them. And they faced—with tired dignity—
the kaleidoscopic sea of faces and lenses and pencils and microphones
and flashing notebooks that stretched ahead of them to infinity across
the floor of the converted hotel ballroom...
with everyone half-dazed by television's shrivelling glare.

*And yet...and yet...my God!...that Dutch correspondent was right...
why drag the families along on these campaign junkets...why subject
them to us press guys...why make them sit there with nothing possible
to say or do but look decent and worthy of being a candidate's
family...they must have heard that speech a zillion times before about
poverty and our injustice to our black brothers and the unending horror
of Viet-Nam...and still they have to sit there and act as though
it's the Gospel itself...just because it's part of the good old American
political custom to drag the family along at election time...
to Hell with it!...let's kill THAT tradition—and get along with
examining the presidential candidates without any supporting cast!*

155

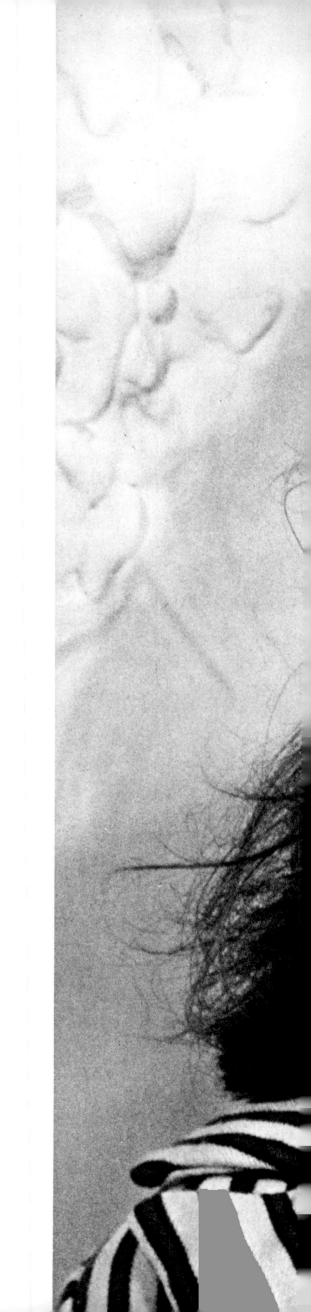

*...hey Senator !...look behind you
...look around beautiful mother...
that child is only thirteen...look
around and you'll take her out of...
why don't I have the guts to stand up
and shout STOP SENATOR!
LET THAT GIRL GET SOME SLEEP!
...campaigning for days...now she's
afraid even to yawn so she won't
embarrass her Dad...looks like a
painting of a Spanish martyr...
but it'll soon be over...and her
Dad won't even know how she felt.*

Senator McGovern used strong, pure colors to paint a word-picture of the people—and nation—he would like to see born of the chaos, heartbreak, hatred, and social conflagration in which we Americans suddenly had found ourselves—a world of reality, not that land of fiction inherited from our ancestors. Phoenix-like, we would rise again from the flames!

Not a correspondent in the room would have faulted the Senator a single syllable in his speech. Still, everyone there would have been equally pleased with a fast, precise sketch of the future's face, instead of getting the whole elaborate masterpiece while those television lights burned holes through one's skull.

And as the Senator spoke, old pro Pierre Salinger never flicked an eye. He simply fired up his cigar, smoothed down his riverboat gambler's sideburns, and searched for familiar faces among those correspondents before him but offered no trace of familiarity in return. There was no shadow of the past—and not the slightest glimpse of the future, anywhere in sight.

160

Then, finally, the press conference ended.

The Democrats surged in for their convention, and every one of them seemingly headed for the great ballrooms of the city's grand old hotels.

When the Californians convened their caucus, to host the party's three major candidates, they assembled in an ornate grotto of the LaSalle, home—surely—of robust blowouts back in those rock-fisted days when railroad lords and cattle barons ruled the town. Now, instead of wild shouts punctuated by perhaps a casual pistol shot into the ceiling, the delegates quietly raised their patient hands, and sat waiting to be heard.

Only two, of the four declared Democratic candidates for President actually mattered in Chicago—with only one of them really having a chance to win.

Somewhere—and nobody seemed to care just where—on the perimeter of the convention city, self-nominating noises were still being heard from that stubborn defender of the southern white man's world—the ax-handle donor from Atlanta—but even fellow Georgians lapsed into awkward silence on the rare occasions when his name was mentioned. On the other side of the coin being flipped in Chicago—and related only by sharing the title of Democrat— Senator George McGovern was making a last-minute bid for his party's nomination...not because he dreamed he might get it—but because he felt duty-bound as an alarmed citizen and a member of our government to speak out on basic issues of national conduct which he felt were threatening our country's future, and, beyond even that, the question of peace in the world.

Of course, no one mentioned the still-reigning President of the United States. He had disappeared into the vastness of his Texas domain (probably planted before his three-network console of television sets), while shunning Chicago.

So—in almost classic American fashion—the convention delegates were being offered their party's champions...a former professor...or former pharmacist. Eugene McCarthy: Minnesota Senator; knight-errant riding upon Viet-Nam. Hubert Humphrey: Vice-President of the Republic; White House heir apparent.

165

Both men—McCarthy, the former professor, and Humphrey, a former pharmacist—seemed locked in a visual *mano-a-mano* across the caucus room. Since his surprise demolition of Lyndon Johnson's career in New Hampshire, McCarthy—a novice in the international arena—had assumed a mantle of pious wisdom implying solution of great issues. His appeal: the "children's" anti-war crusade. Humphrey—an ever-ready talker, prone to tears; a chrome-tough fighter of our "liberal wars," now tagged "conservative"—was impaled upon compromising LBJ's legacy, or his own destiny.

Open conflict flashed across the Amphitheater floor when the Convention Chairman, Carl Albert—supported by Platform Chairman Hale Boggs—attempted to blast anti-war delegates down into their seats. But those hecklers were not kookie-yippie-hippie-professorial-draft-card-burning-anti-Viet-Nam-war fanatics. They were fully accredited Democratic delegates to their national convention, and they'd be ------------- if any ------------- would use platform microphones to out-gun them! The protesters had made earlier—private—demands that the

party Platform be written to include a specific anti-Viet-Nam war plank reflecting the sentiments of many delegates standing in direct opposition to the Administration's Viet-Nam policy, which, they felt, jeopardized the country's honor. Chairmen Albert and Boggs —even with microphones—were shouted into frustrated silence.

And so they glared and thundered at each other about our national role in Viet-Nam, while a few miles away other men watched them as silent spectators—men who rarely discussed war with strangers.

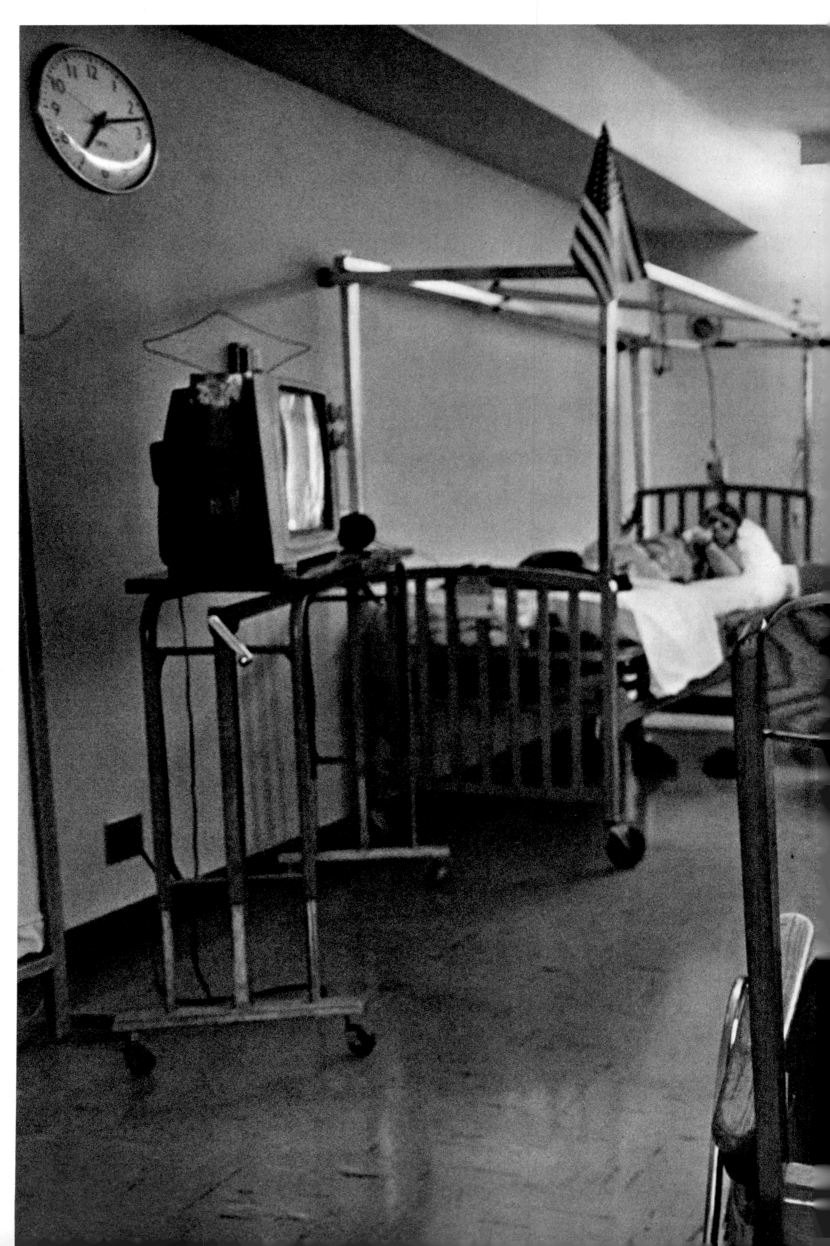

Every night of the Democratic convention, an attentive group of young men— all with time on their hands— listened, and, when they could, watched those older men who were fighting for control of the nation's future—and the Presidency.

Thirty-two miles straight north of the Chicago Amphitheater— an easy hour by the expressway— twelve hundred and sixty-three Marines, and a scattering of paratroopers, filled the beds and wards of the Great Lakes naval hospital.

In one ward, though favoring their old buddy, Alfie Neuman, for President, they realized an outsider might be nominated. Still, they wished they'd done more campaigning for *their* candidate. But, of course, that was nearly impossible— since they all were in traction, or amputees.

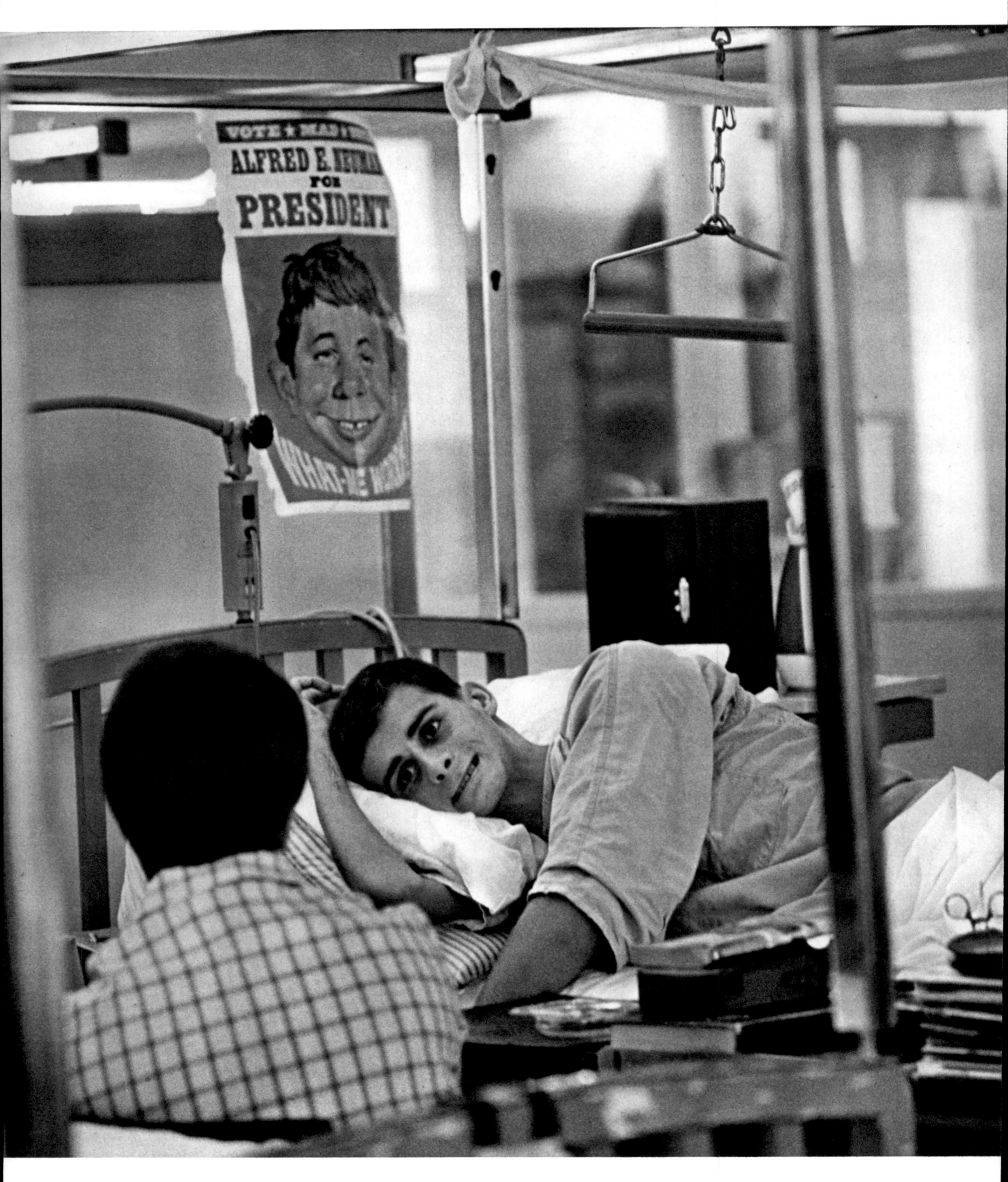

When a man's wife or girl came visiting, everyone else in the ward immediately left to visit another buddy down along the corridor, unless—for many of them—it was still a bit too early to try learning how to walk again. Then, they would turn and quietly watch an evening TV western, or the convention; or, if just in from 'Nam, they lay sprawled amongst snowy feathers; great, slender-legged, shot-down tropical water birds…while one of those always-anonymous, always-present, always-good visiting artists sketched a portrait to be sent back home. No one—ever—watched the other amputee, with his teen-age wife.

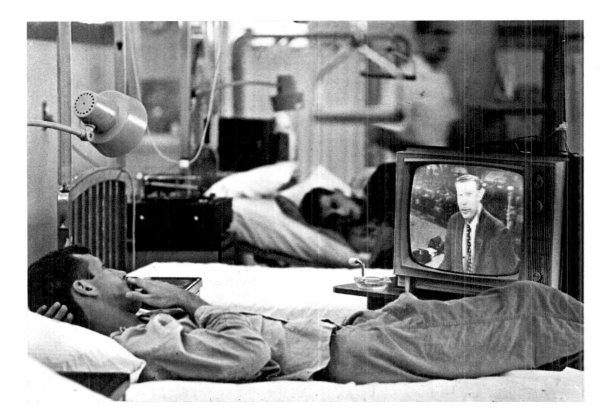

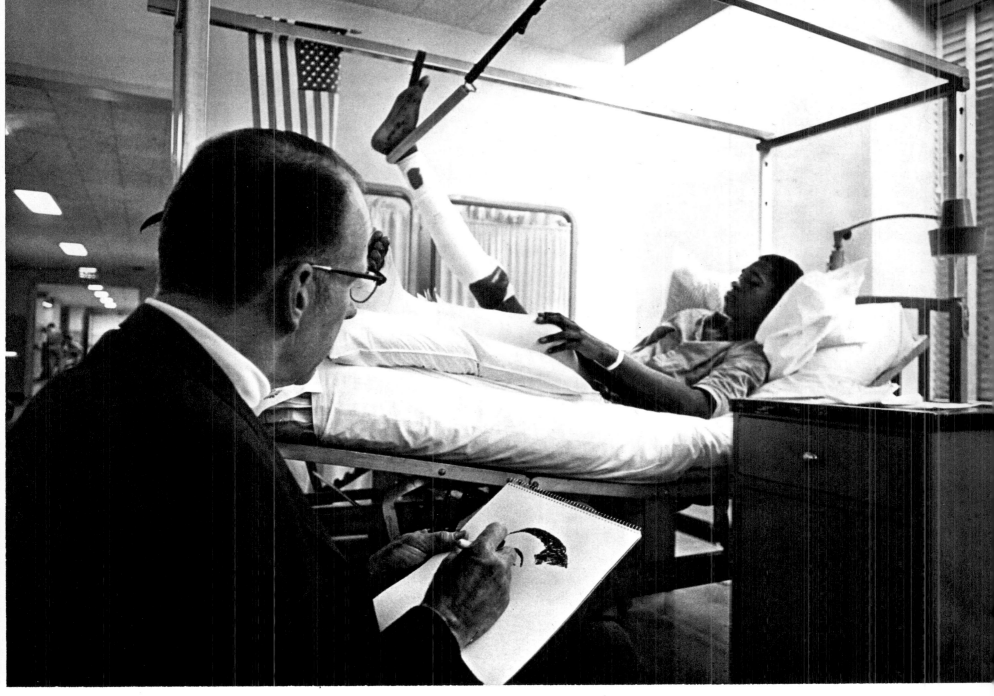

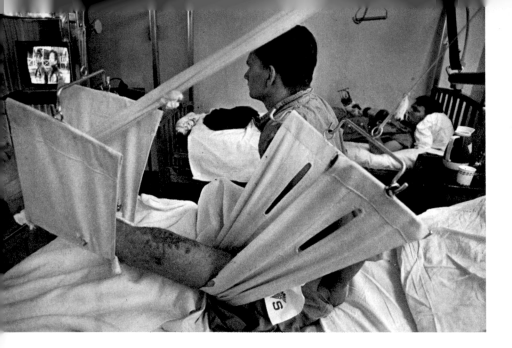

The hospitalized veterans from Viet-Nam, those bandaged
men already ambulatory, or in wheelchairs—not the newly
arrived, of course, with wounds still draining and legs
and arms suspended in traction slings which made turning,
or sleeping, or practicing exercises awkward—watched the
convention and anti-war demonstrations without comment.
No rancor…no recriminations…no second-guessing combat
strategy…no contempt for hippies, no matter how unshorn;
hatred for flag-burners…no judgements on policy-makers,
a world so remote from their own as to be nearer fiction;
like the western being watched by that grunt down the ward.
Then, there were the blind, broken, burned, who saw nothing.

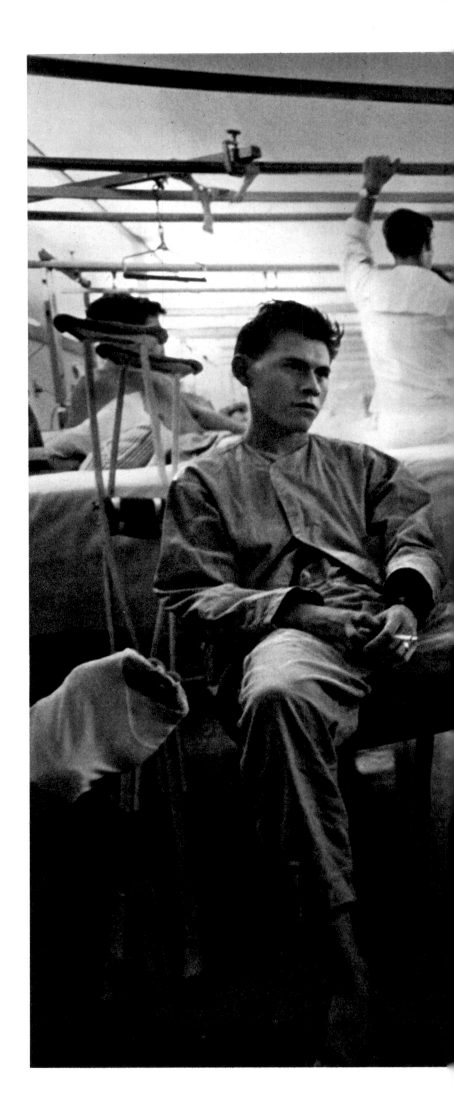

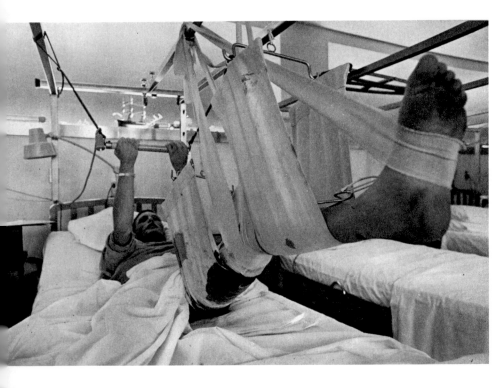

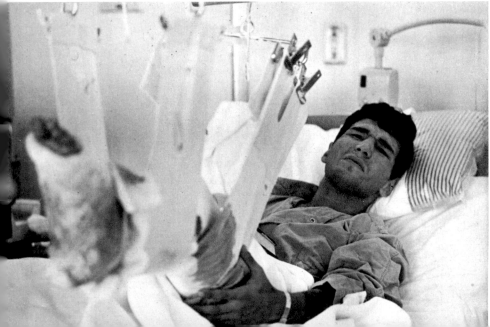

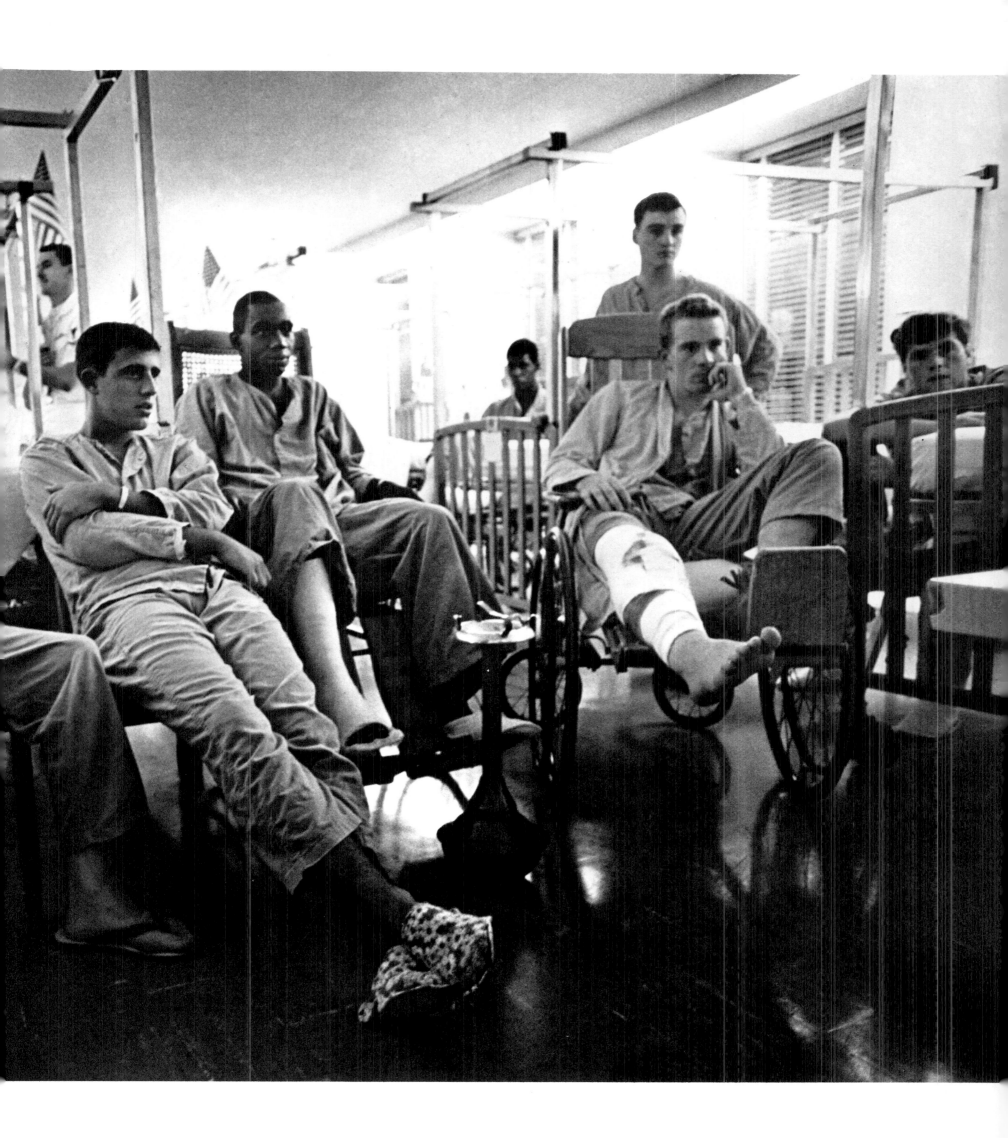

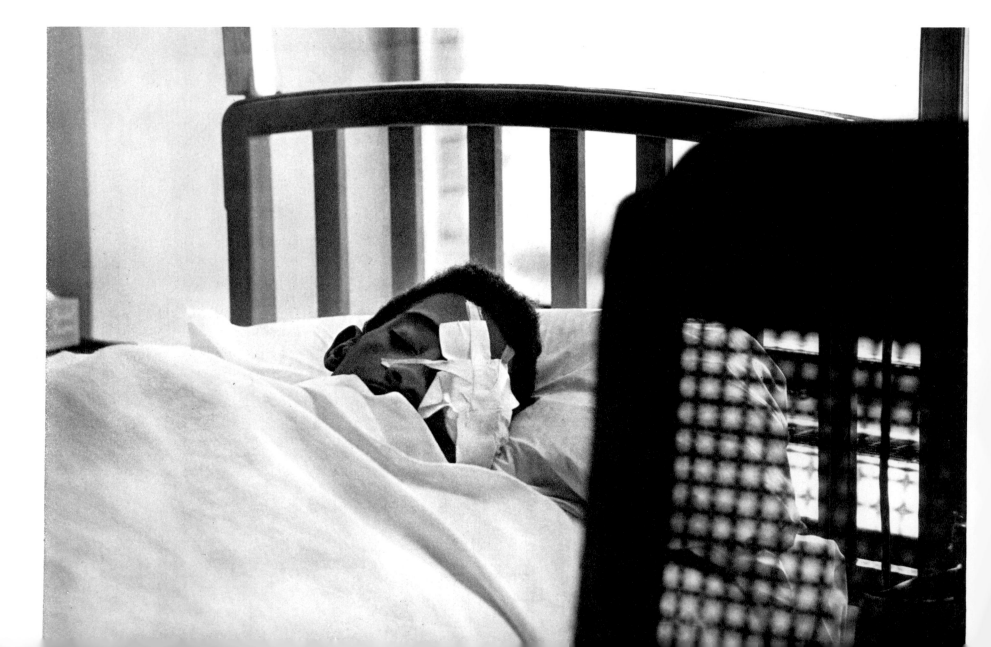

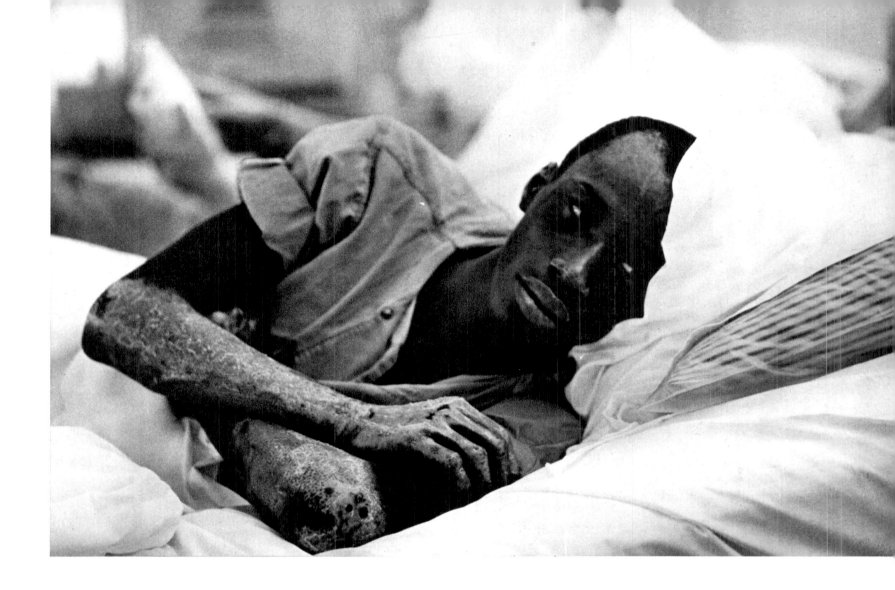

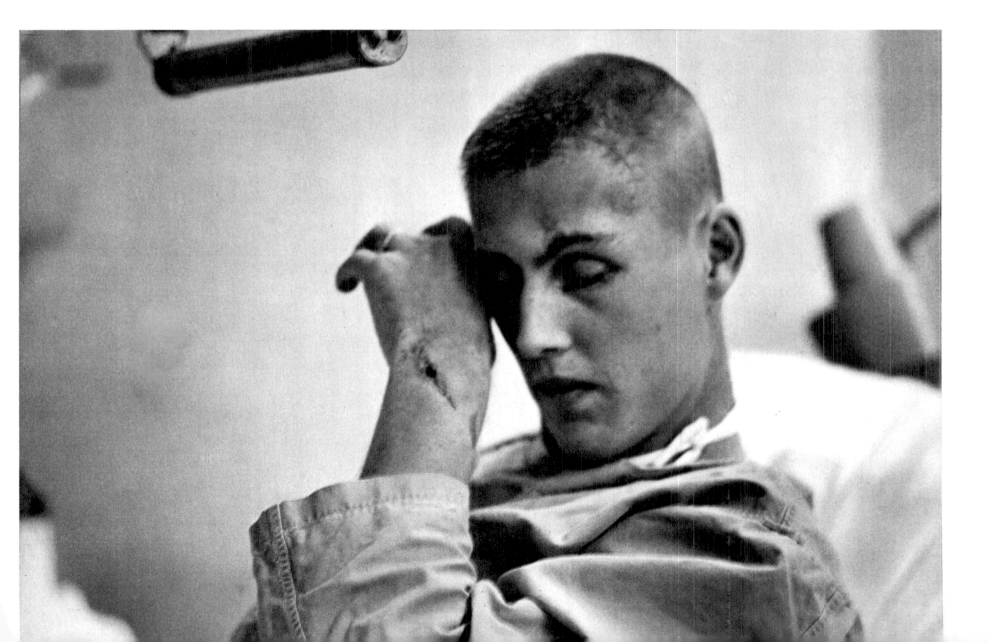

During the same days that the nation's politicians met in
conventions to present their party Platforms and to nominate
their choices for the next commander-in-chief of all of our
armed forces, the staffs of the nation's military hospitals
were trying to accommodate and administer to the needs of
the wounded men who flowed into their wards from Viet-Nam.
These were the men—invariably referred to by politicians as
"our boys"—the plaster-encased, melancholia-enshrouded,
pain-enduring men, so dear to the conventioneers and their war.

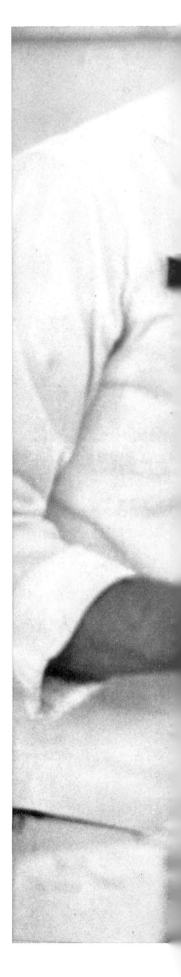

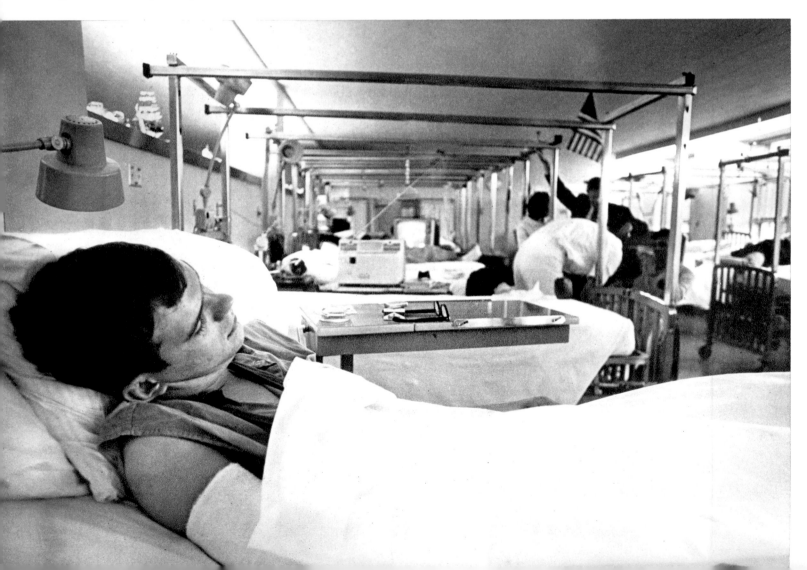

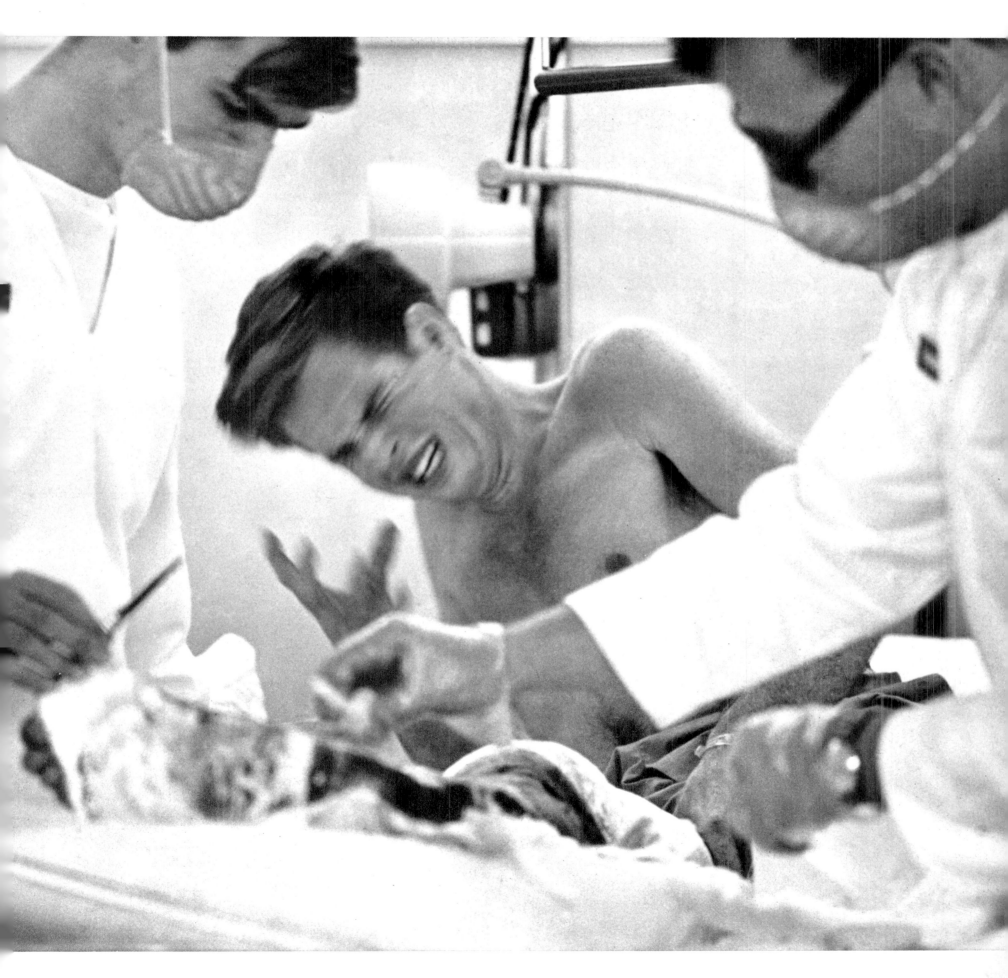

Oblivious to the convention, a Marine...born in Mason, Ohio, but more recently of a mortar-torn rice paddy near Da Nang, South Viet-Nam... lurched upright but without a sound, his face shrieking in agony, as hospital orderlies dug fragments of bone and bomb from his shattered leg. The Marine was already half-immune to pain-killing drugs.

During the torture, he looked up to ask a single question: "Okay, Doc, tell me straight. You think maybe I'll lose it?" "No!" He stared down at the flayed wreckage on the sheet.

While he was being treated, other Marines saw my camera: "Yuhoo—Hero! Hey Smitty! Wow...that's a good one! You tryin' to get an Academy Award Oscar, with that face?" Voices of men without arms, legs, eyes; or in their thick plaster shells—the voices of fallen men with Purple Hearts.

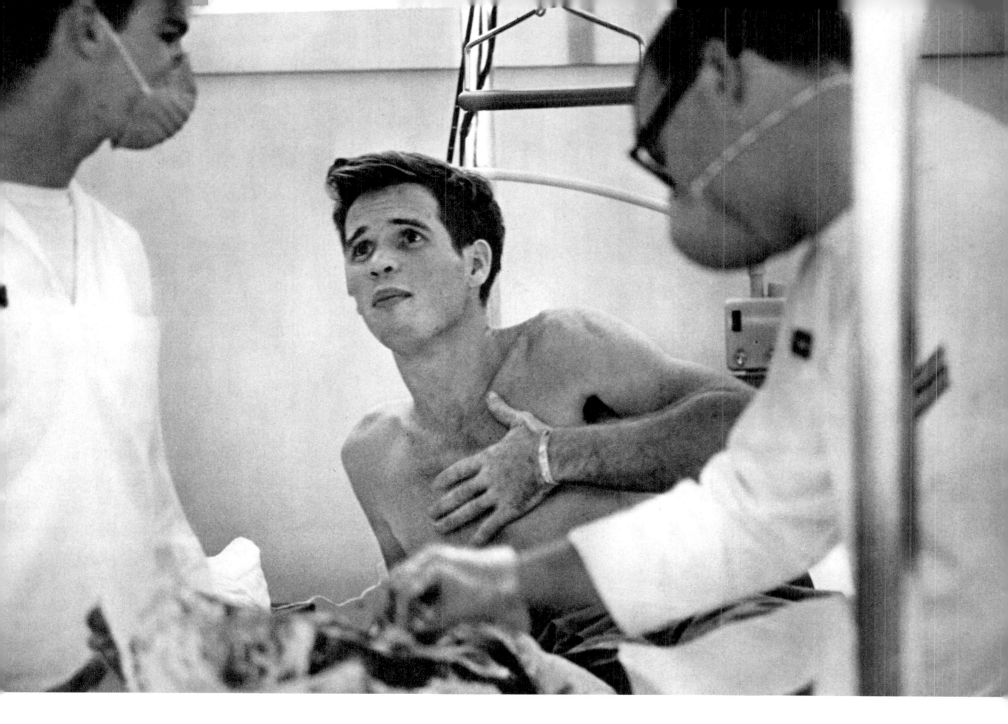

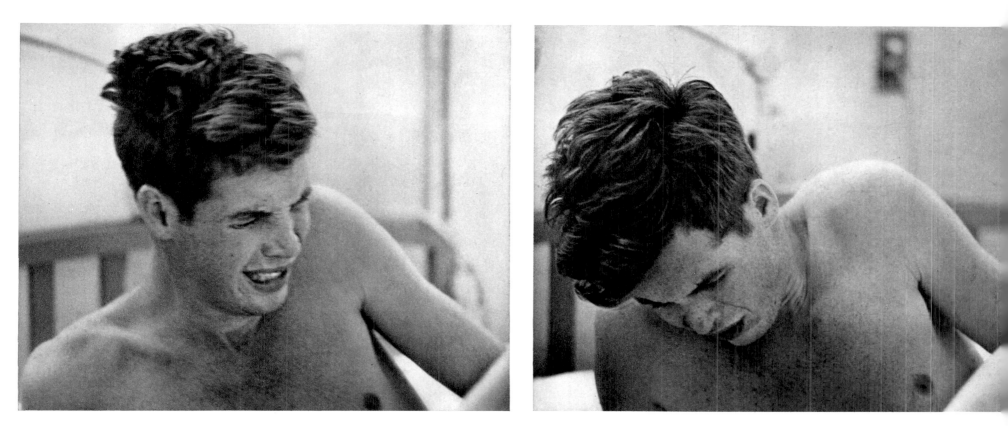

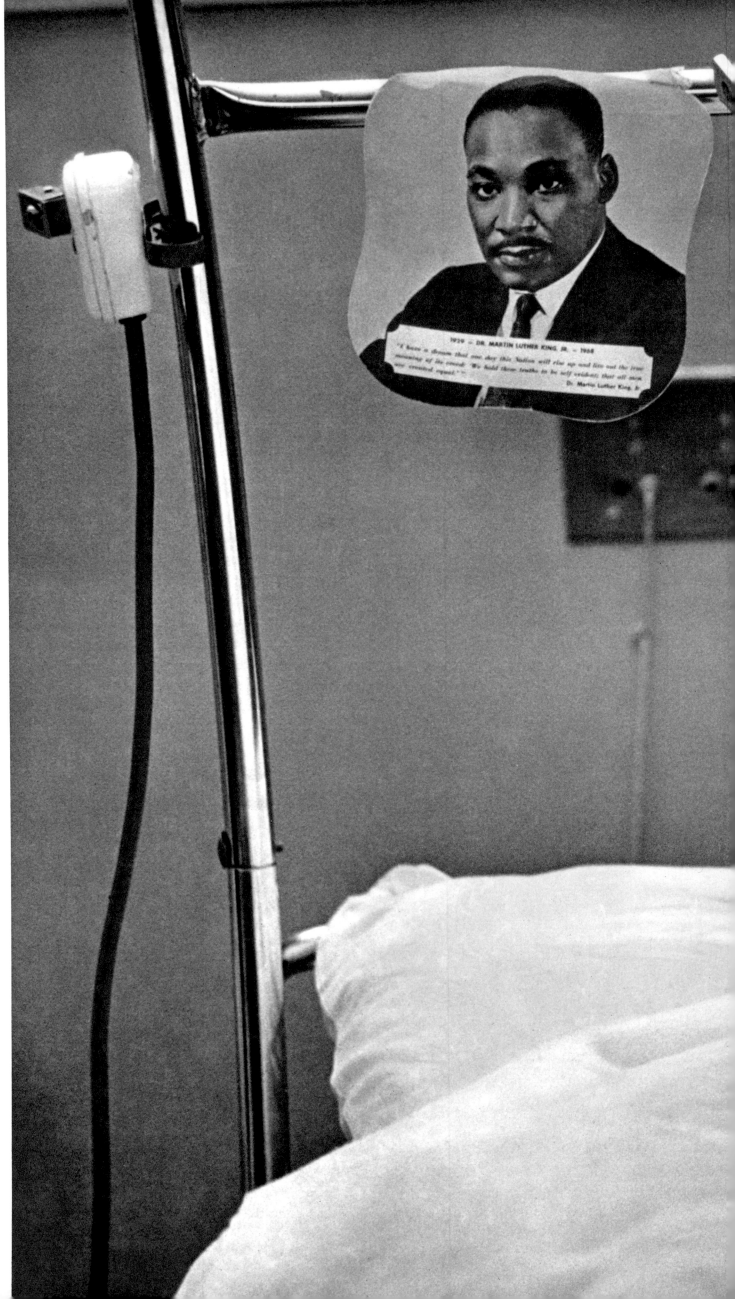

Marines in the next ward whispered, not sure whether he was asleep, or under new sedation: "Don't forget our 101st paratrooper... Don't forget the Major!"

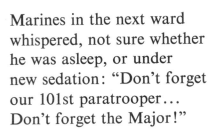

"POSITION CHANGES

Front	– 0001	– 0100
R-Side	– 0100	– 0500
Back	– 0500	– 0800
Front	– 0800	– 0900
L-Side	– 0900	– 1200
Front	– 1200	– ..... "

Night and day, until he makes the Big Jump itself: totally paralyzed below his neck and shoulders.

Turning to leave the ward, I asked the night duty-officer an obvious question: "How many delegates or candidates, Democrats or Republicans, have come here to visit with these men?" He looked across their beds, then switched off the light. "Not one."

184

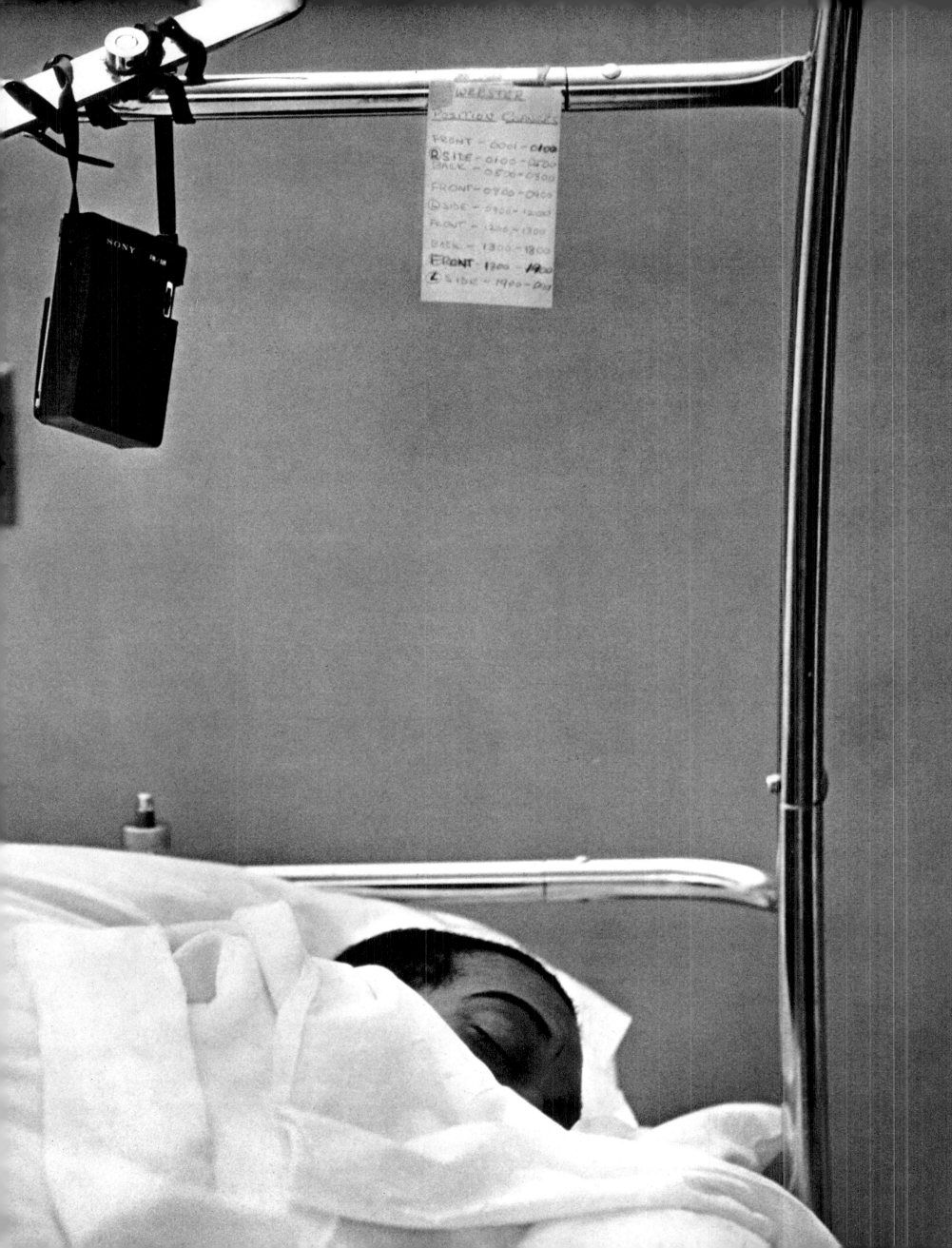

Senator Eugene McCarthy's
Chicago youth headquarters
was a forlorn second-floor
garret over a beer parlor,
behind the Conrad Hilton.
During the convention it
became Mecca for fanatically
devout, idealistic, mostly
innocent, usually college-
age protest groups making
their political pilgrimage.

They, too, marched under
Churchill's V-for-victory
war standard. But, now,
there was no Atlantic Wall
lying in the mists ahead;
no malignant necklace
of squat, flak-tower warts
to burn away; no hulking
Fortress Europe looming
silent—waiting. Without
such barricades to conquer,
victory, over almost any
adversary, seemed like
a real bargain—at $ 2.00!

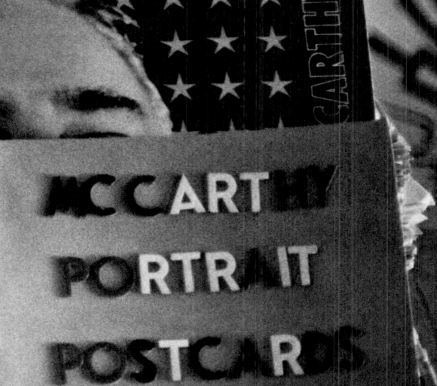

Volunteer McCarthy workers arrived from every-where, instant-enthusiasm bubbling in their wakes. Young students, young mothers, young Chinese, Jews, Catholics, protesting Protestants of all sects, all colors, a few hippies, one grandmother, a broken-necked coordinator, actors, army boots, painters, enough musicians for Carnegie Hall, no bare feet, rucksacks, paper sacks, matched Gucci bags, sign-plastered Mustang convertibles, sandwich boards on sweating thin shoulders, a solitaire pearl at the throat of one Portuguese-linen blouse, and amateur clowns bass-drumming the city for gifts to an empty campaign chest...

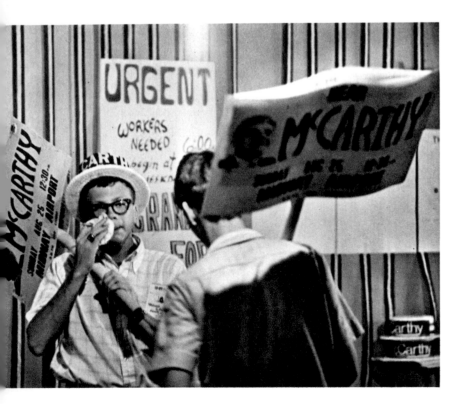

...everyone inflamed with the vision of that First Crusade of American youth was there; except their knight.
He stayed aloof in his tower of the Conrad Hilton, never walking amongst his troops.

She was out in the streets
with stars in her eyes,
the night
their dream-bubble burst...

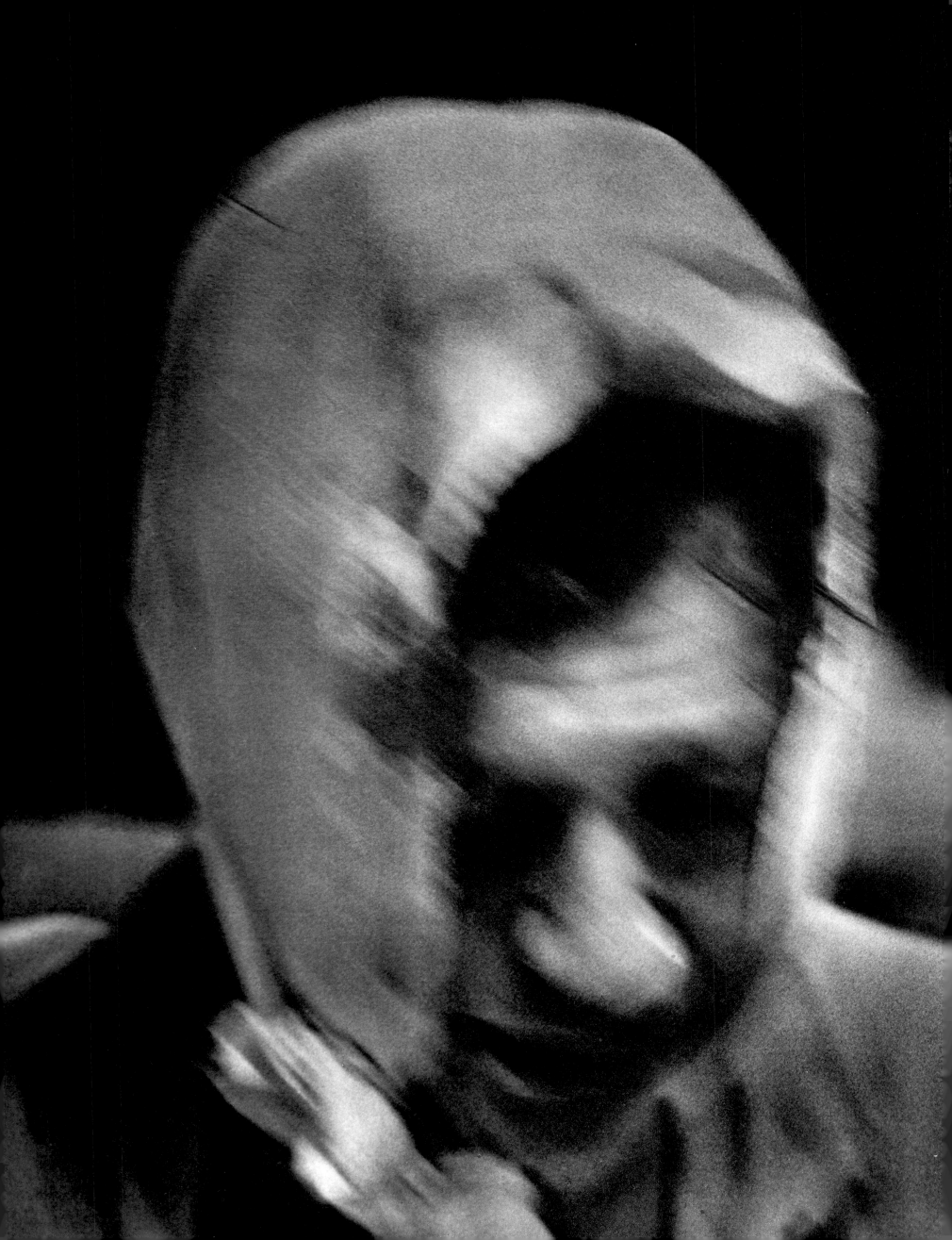

McCarthy-kids...hippies...yippies
...TV commentators...bystanders...
press photographers, and anybody
else caught in that first charge
went down to their knees, or
upon their faces, or backs—
down.. flat down...split-scalps
down.. broken-nosed down...
smashed-cameras down—
battered there by the
full-swinging billy clubs
of Mayor Richard J. Daley's
Chicago riot police,
who'd finally gotten a
bellyful of yippies, hippies,
McCarthy-kids, protesters, and
professors; and probably the
whole convention itself, with its
demands of around-the-clock
protection of delegates while
coddling a cityful of taunting,
oath-and-junk hurling,
jargon-chanting, long-haired
crackpots who'd soon go
back home leaving the cops with
a town that was a beauty of a
just-cooled, murder-stewing volcano
even before the convention opened.
So the cops "rioted."

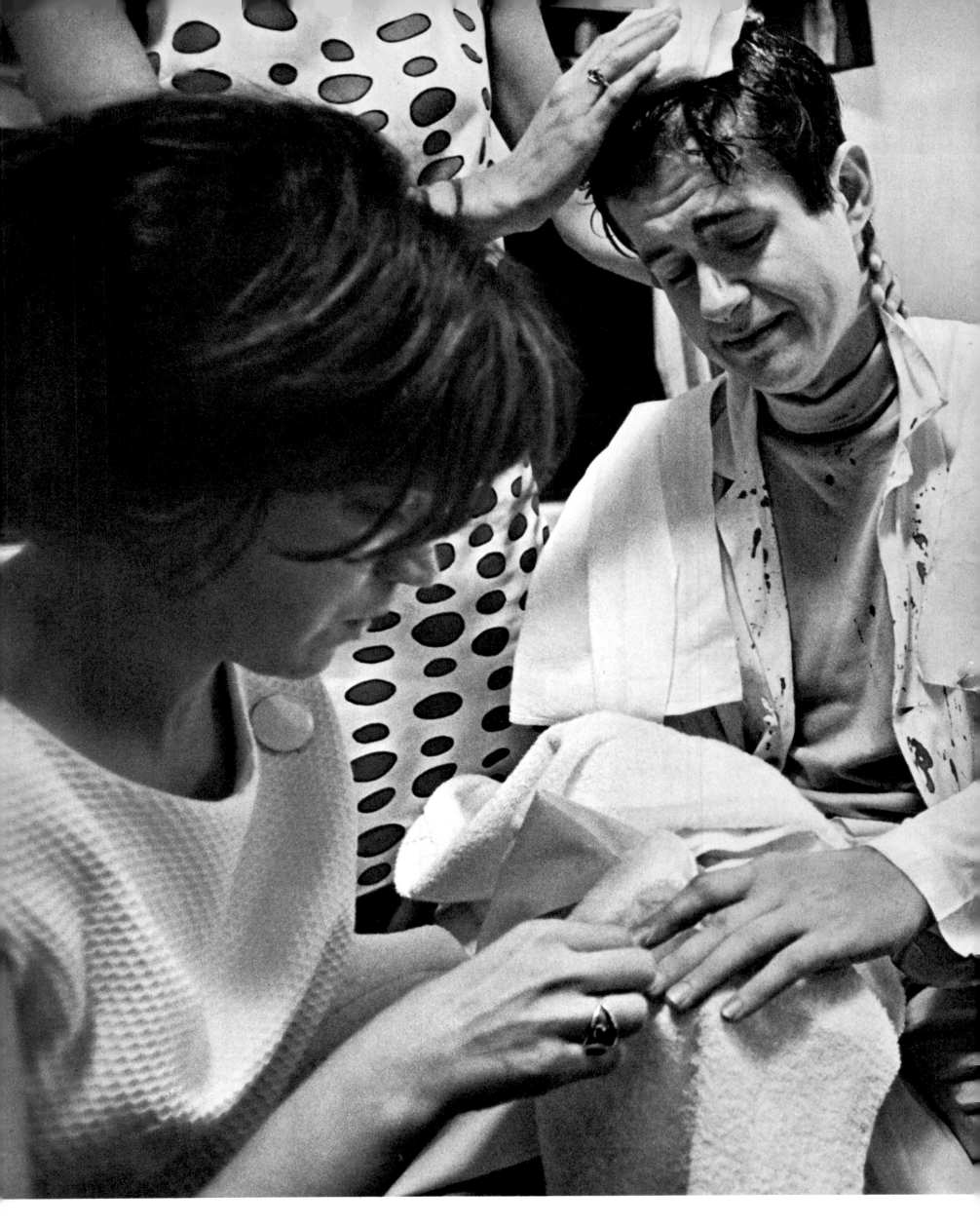

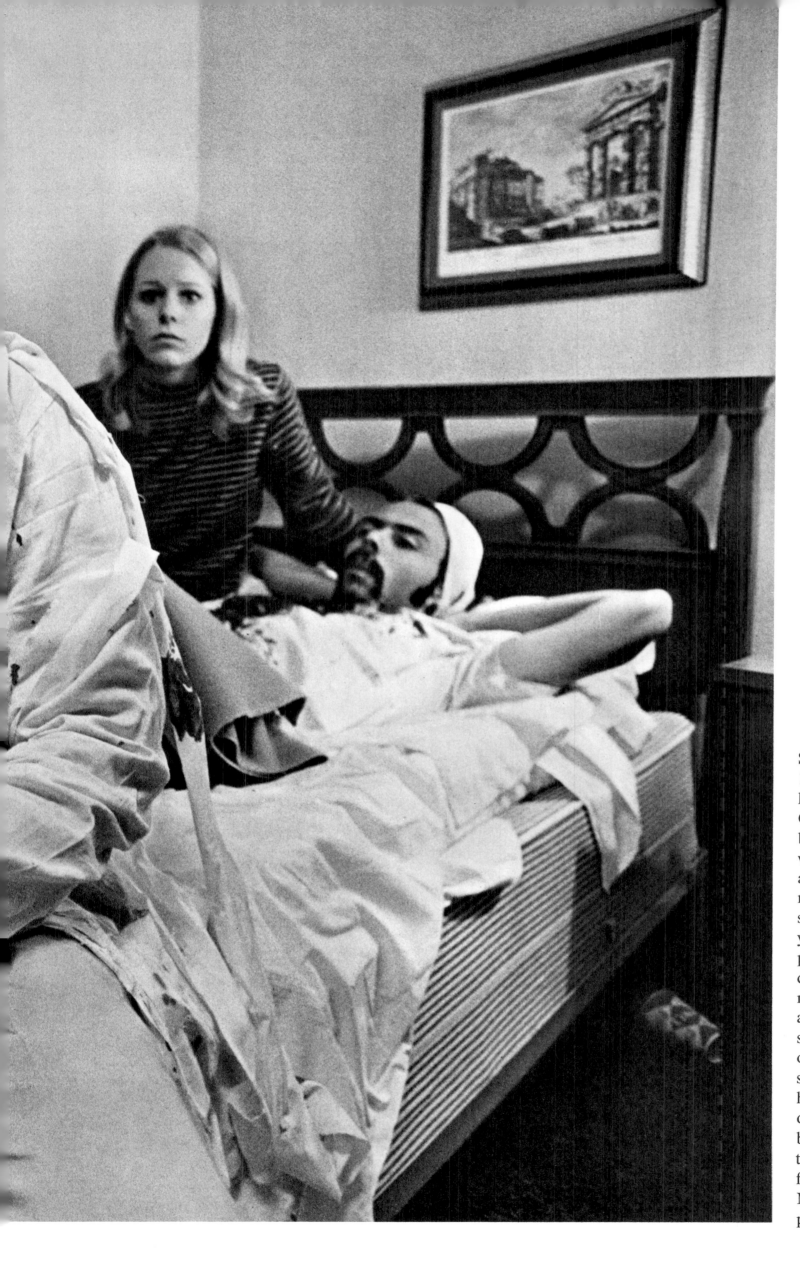

Senator McCarthy's 15th-floor campaign headquarters in the Conrad Hilton Hotel became a hospital within minutes after assault echelons of riot police in the street below clubbed youth volunteers, pressmen, bearded demonstrators of many categories, and those bystanders so foolish as to come on a summer evening stroll to the Hilton, hoping to see some of the "fun" that had been dominating the television news shows for nearly a week. Now, they too were part of the program.

One group of McCarthy-girls kneeling
in a corridor looked like they
were fitting a friend's wedding dress.
They were ripping hotel sheets
to make bandages for wounded workers
sprawled upon beds everywhere,
or just sitting stunned on the floor.

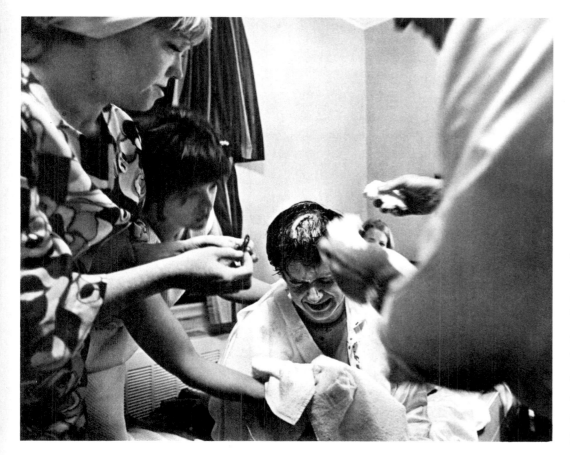

The McCarthy-kids quickly learned how to stop the flow of blood; how to shave and then patch battered skulls; how to wrap and tape the head and leg wounds which constituted the majority of injuries. Yet, at the same time, a strange mixture of outrage and curiosity drew them to television sets on that 15th floor. There, instead of watching the Democrats' nomination-night balloting at the Amphitheater, they saw a delayed television news program of friends being clubbed on Michigan Avenue —just below their hotel rooms—where shouts of demonstrators, again taunting the police, filled the dulcet summer-night air of Chicago.

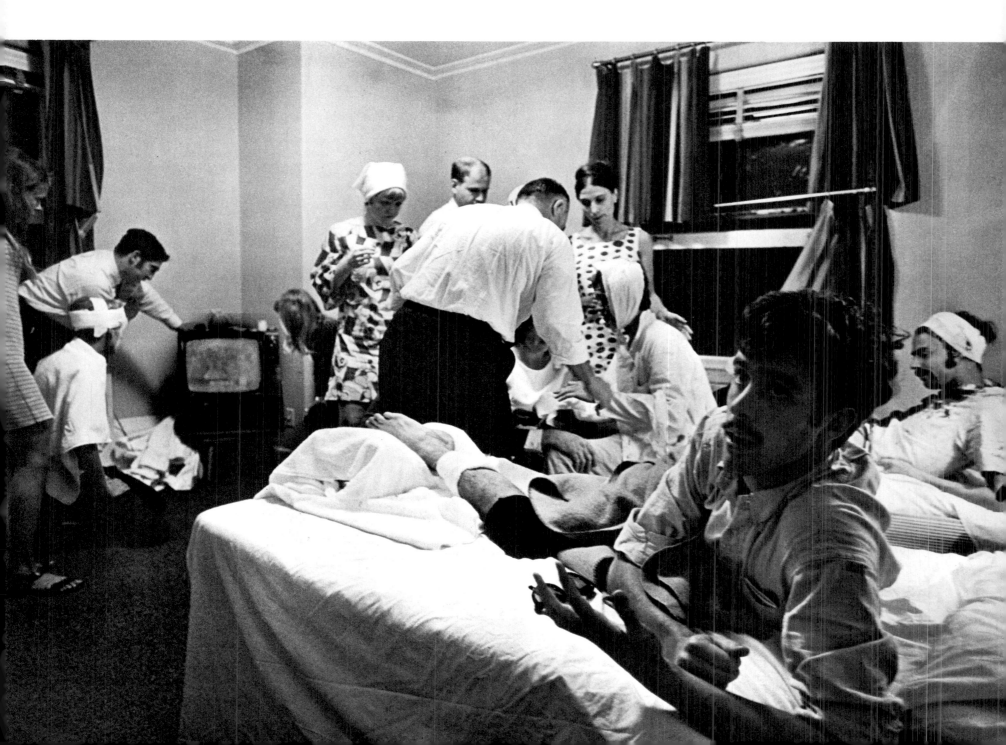

Few, among Senator McCarthy's volunteers,
had ever been involved in any sort of confrontation
with the police, especially riot police—burly,
combat-helmeted, mace-spraying, club-swinging professionals—
men accustomed to dealing with other near-professionals
from a city's ghettoes, or strike-bound factories; or,
during ordinary work days in a city like Chicago,
facing the gangster underworld itself.

For them—the pros—dealing with the convention hecklers
was simply a matter of ordering one attack,
moving in fast with clubs flailing, then tossing the
demonstrators into paddy wagons or ambulances...
those who didn't escape into side streets,
or the semi-sanctuary of the Conrad Hilton Hotel lobby.

As TV cameramen saturated the room with drama,
I watched the young McCarthy volunteers
—those innocent American boy-men—
watch friends being beaten in the street below:
fists clenched; lips half-bitten in rage;
mouths agape at the unknown sight of raw,
savage violence...tears moistening eye lashes
...breath coming only in short gasps.
And I found some difficulty in relating them
to the hundreds of silent, wounded men lying
in their hospital wards only an hour's drive from
the Conrad Hilton—but an entire world apart.
And yet, I also wondered whether these boy-men's
world wasn't equally as filled with honor,
and just as valid, in the end.

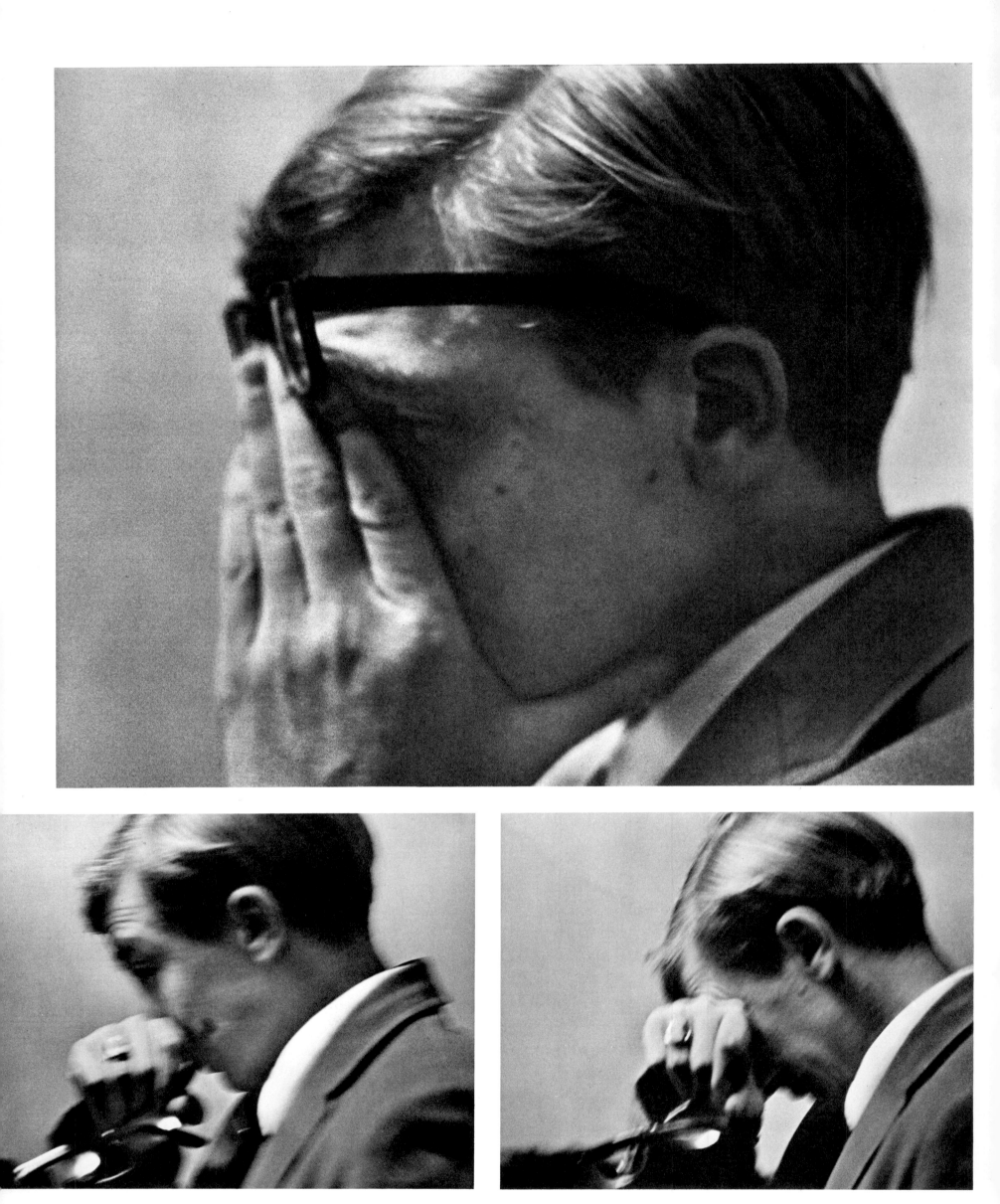

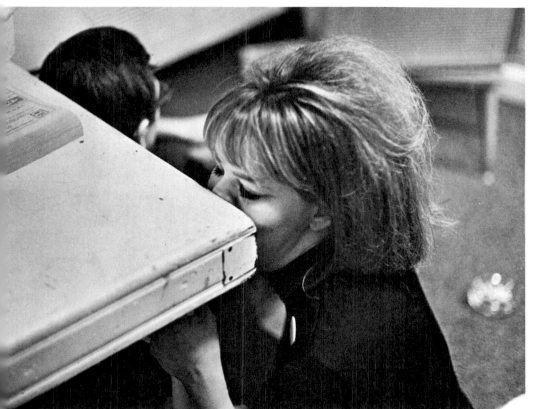

The police clean-up of demonstrators
lasted about half an hour.
For the shocked warriors of Senator McCarthy's
"Youth Crusade," television's coverage
must have appeared to run forever.

A softly crying girl sank to her knees,
unable to endure the sight or sound of billy clubs
thudding upon also crying, unprotected
heads—against a muffled, distant chant of
"pigs…pigs…pigs…pigs…sieg heil!…sieg heil!
…pigs…sieg heil!…pigs…pigs…"
Then, she looked up at me—pleadingly.
"Tell it like it was…*please* tell it like it was!"
She buried her face in a telephone table, sobbing.
It did not cease even when another stricken
crusader knelt, and tried to comfort her.

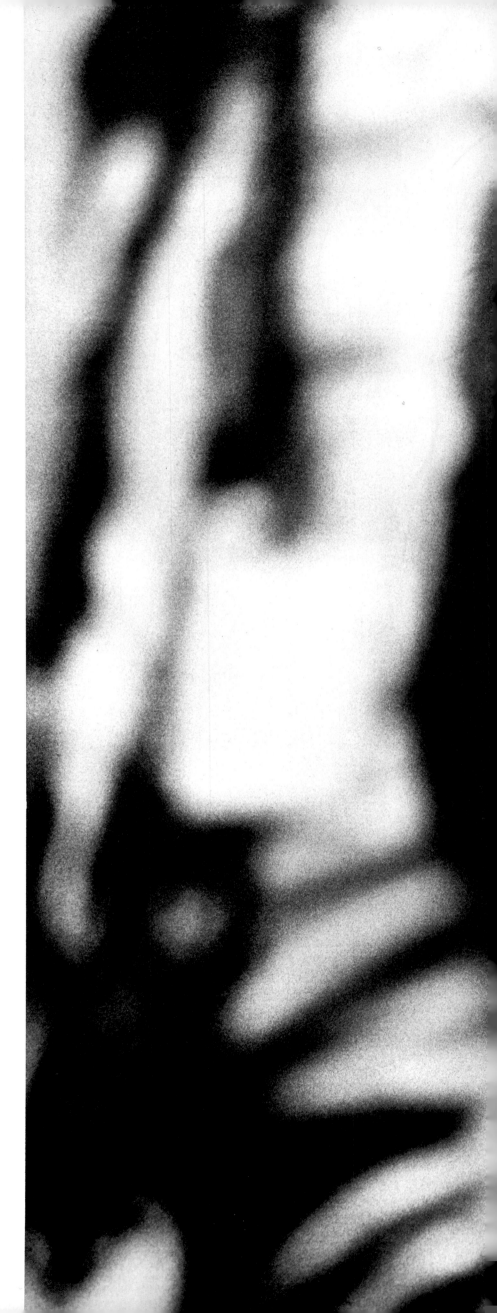

All of this world's tears,
from whatever source, lay shimmering in one pair of eyes.

McCarthy-girls...mostly college students...who only an hour
earlier had been submerged in nomination-night frenzy,
suddenly found themselves serving as nurses, mothers, and
wartime comrades for their bludgeoned friends, who had staggered
or been carried back to Senator McCarthy's headquarters floor.
They were generally drenched with blood; head to waist.
In that moment, the girls achieved womanhood—magnificently.

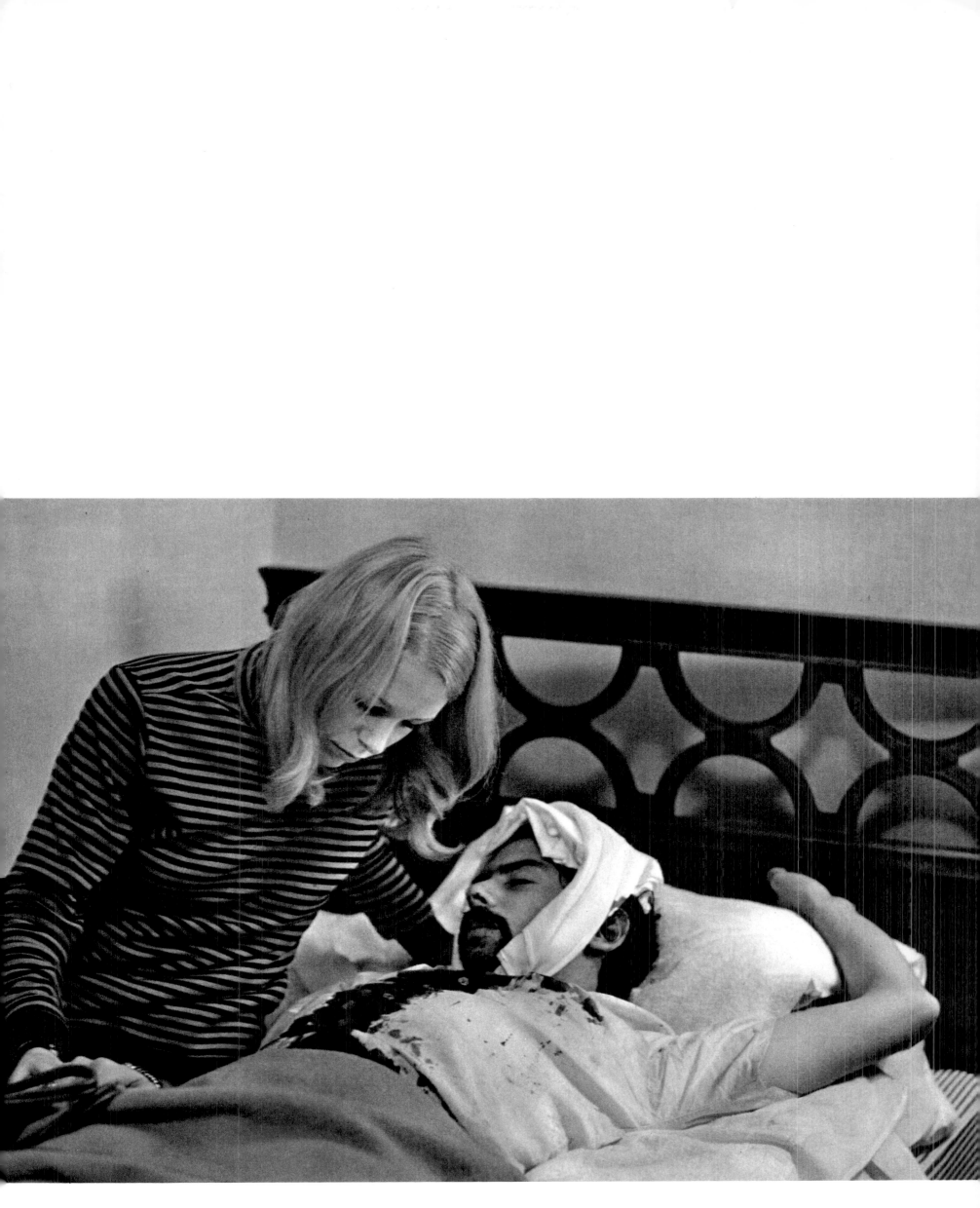

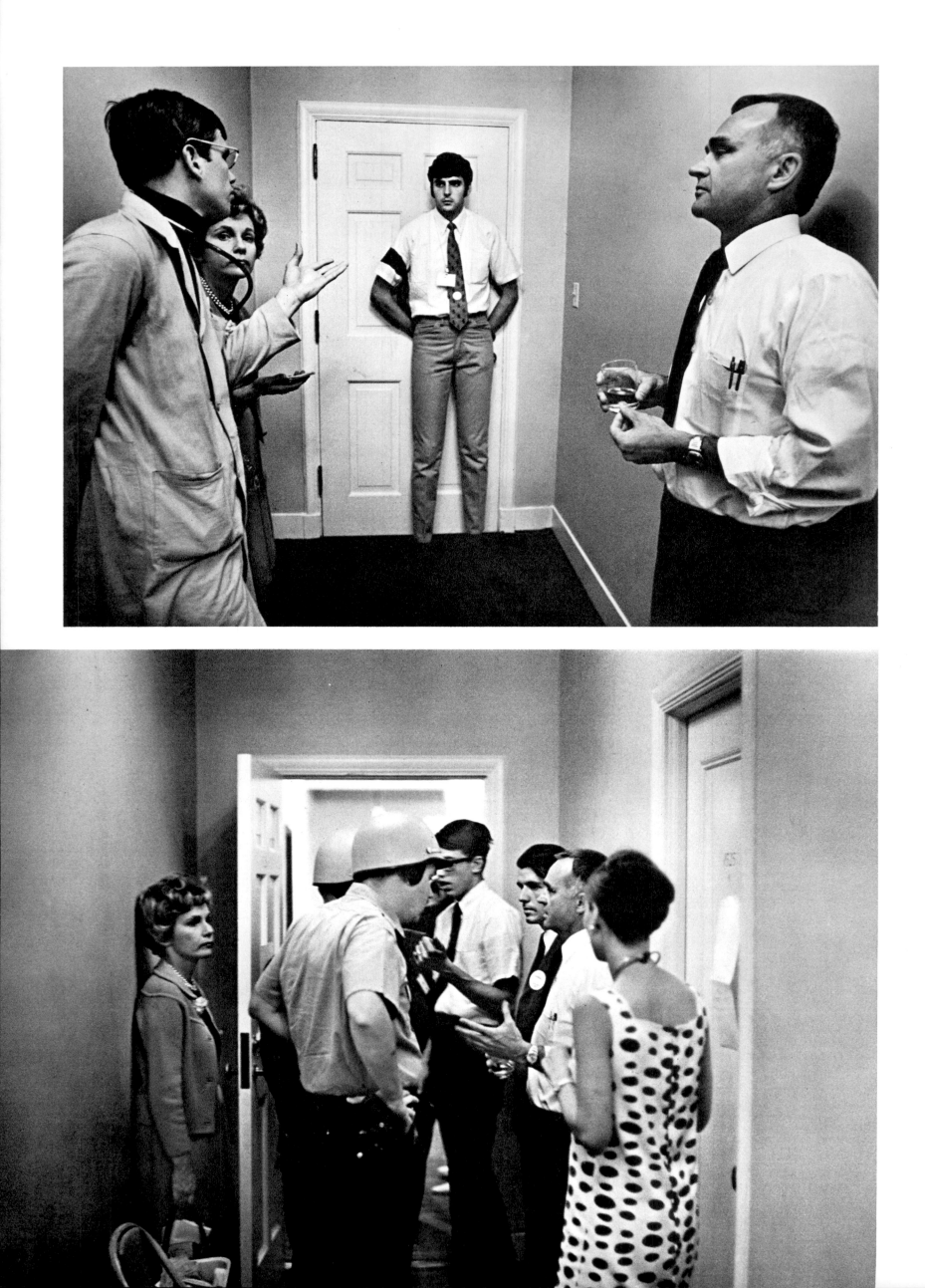

Senator McCarthy's doctor took immediate command of the
emergency. It was obvious that several of the injured needed
hospital examination and care. The nearest ambulances were
those of the police, who soon arrived with stretchers. Their way
was barred until assurances were given that the wounded would
indeed be taken to the hospital—not headquarters. It took
audacity and courage to parlay with the police—armed only
with the black sleeve bands that had appeared with the beatings:
"mourning the death of the Democratic party." And the girl
crusaders accompanied their bloodied young warriors into the
night, bound for who-knew-where in the enemy citadel.
Courageous, too! But, when compared with student-police
wars in Paris—Tokyo—Madrid—Mexico City...crushed skulls...
gouged eyeballs...fractured spines...or shot dead, the riot
police hit hard, yet with restraint—professionals against rank
amateurs—in that *first* big confrontation at the barricades.

McCarthy's laconic bid for the Democratic nomination had been rejected, his Youth Crusade shattered—its warriors routed or wounded—by the time the first, and final, ballot was tallied down at the stockyards Amphitheater. Hubert Horatio Humphrey was to be the party candidate; so ordained almost from the start.

As they flowed from the night
and on into the night,
they radiated a light of their own.

The protest marchers stopped at Grant Park, in front of the Conrad Hilton.
Quietly singing, they sat upon what once had been grass; long ago—a week before.
Their gondola lanterns were nothing but simple waxed-paper drinking cups,
shielding candles. One of their crusader-marching songs was well woven
into the history of the nation: "The Battle Hymn of the Republic."
Their miniature American flags belonged to everyone, too.
But two songs were special unto themselves.
"We Shall Overcome"—borrowed from a good man: Martin Luther King.
Then, they sang a ballad I had never heard before.
"Where Have All The Flowers Gone?...where have all
our young girls gone?...where have all our soldiers gone?..."
I can answer that question about soldiers—and Marines!
But I wish someone would ask me: Where have all our photographers gone—
our old war photographers? Oh, how I'd love to answer:
"One of them has come here to join you!"

Somewhere—far from the ballot-counting McCarthyites, who were wounded even more deeply than those hammered flat by the police—another forlorn figure must also have been watching the convention, which fell on his sixtieth birthday. Though he was the leader of his assembled party—and President of the United States—he stayed far away from Chicago, yet another victim of that tragic, historic week.

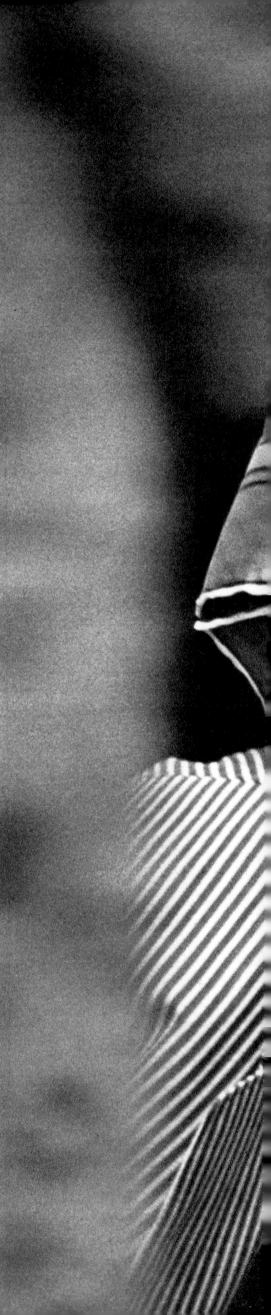

It didn't take them long
to wrap up the debris of dreams,
at the Conrad Hilton
discothèque headquarters
of Senator Eugene McCarthy.

Gene McCarthy

A single spot-
light neatly
haloed his
classic head.
Gene McCarthy
was no longer
a candidate—
his anguished,
self-assigned
crusade, dead.

Bells *did* toll,
for now it was
midnight...
the wake had
already begun.

Hubert Humphrey had been nominated for President...
Eugene McCarthy had conceded defeat...
George McGovern had made his point, and garnered a few votes...
That ax-handle donor from Georgia had—it really didn't matter...
The cordon of Chicago policemen had withdrawn from in front of the Conrad Hilton
following their "riot," being replaced by battle-geared, tear-gas loaded infantrymen
of the Illinois National Guard; flanked by a covey of light-machine gun jeeps.
Others, with barbed-wire mob-control snouts blocked Michigan Avenue,
as busloads of delegates returned to the hotel.
Except for Humphrey's acceptance speech and introduction of Edmund Muskie,
his Vice-Presidential choice, the Democratic National Convention was finished—
forgetting those black arm-banded, V-for-victory, stubborn crusaders...

The final anti-Viet-Nam war marchers
started far away, beyond the perimeter of
lights surrounding the Conrad Hilton.
Their songs sifted down through the pre-
dawn darkness of Michigan Avenue, into
the streets of a listening city that should
have been sleeping. They walked together,
in front of the night, serene, gently flowing,
a river irresistible in its watershed strength.
Gondola lanterns bobbed downstream
tossing light out into the gloom, and into
the solemn face of each gondolier-crusader.
Many were middle-aged: priests, housewives,
business executives, convention delegates,
ministers, rabbis. Others were young:
students, veterans just out of Viet-Nam, and
draft protesters. Black...brown...bearded
...white...clean-shaven...bald—America
marshalling in the night. And I thought:
If these be the enemy...anarchists...hippies
...terrorists...arsonists—bless them!
And, together, we'll start again tomorrow,
to build something even finer from the ashes.

227

They came, and protested, and sang
their ballads armed with paper lanterns,
miniature flags, their borrowed songs,
and their borrowed sign for victory.
They walked against tear gas, clubs,
barbed-wire jeeps, and soldiers with
automatic rifles and machine guns.
They also came and marched with their
anger, with their convictions, and
with their youth—which they will need.
To conquer, with dreams, takes time.

D.D.D. / CHICAGO / LEICAFLEX SL TELYT 400MM PHOTO: DAVID HOLLANDER / NBC

PHOTO DATA & AFTERTHOUGHTS

It's infrequent, indeed, that a professional photographer feels grateful to a single piece of equipment for gaining what he feels was a momentary jump on his colleagues during the shooting of a highly competitive assignment. Usually, it is the idea, or execution, of a story-theme that hits pay-dirt, first with one's own sense of accomplishment and professional pride, and then with the editors. Since most of us use approximately the same gear, we all head for a story from the same starting box. The guy or girl with the sharpest eye, fastest hand, or clearest concept of the story's mainstream issue wins out. Unless, of course, one simply lucks into *the* shot, and then the rest of us see it and appreciate it for what it delivers—never quite sure whether the other character out-thought us, out-shot us…or, out-lucked us. That's "photojournalism," as I know it.

My assignment by NBC News to shoot a daily television spot during the national conventions at Miami Beach and Chicago provided—for me—the shining exception, where one lens helped me beyond all measure. I'd returned earlier in the year from visiting the Marines at Khe Sanh, hand-carrying my undeveloped films straight to *Life's* darkrooms in New York for souping and printing an essay which closed the day after my arrival, as did an ABC-TV Special documentary. Due to the nature of my leaving Khe Sanh—by-passing Saigon and hardly stopping in Da Nang where all my equipment was stored—I arrived Stateside in battle garb and practically without cameras. Replacing clothing was easy, but I still was almost destitute of cameras when Reuven Frank, President of NBC News, suggested the conventions as a revolutionary project for us both.

Never having attended a presidential convention—in fact, never having shot a professional story in the United States—but being familiar with the general setup, I knew that I would be dependent upon a major-length telephoto lens if I hoped to knock off a series of faces that would give a semi-insight into the functioning of the politicians themselves. I figured there would be a lot of characters loaded with cameras roaming around as lost as myself hoping for something a bit different. I scouted New York among my manufacturer friends, searching for a long lens that was light enough on a single-lens reflex to be hand-held even in the crush of floor activities at each convention. I wanted to shoot my super-closeups from 50–100 feet, without a tripod.

E. Leitz, Inc. in New York all but handed me the conventions on a silver platter when they loaned me a Leicaflex SL, fitted with what might be described with considerable understatement as the sharpest, lightest, easiest-to-focus telephoto lens with which I am familiar—the Leitz Telyt 400mm, f/6.8. It is also one of the slowest, aperture-wise, but I really didn't care. It is a lens that was designed for the 1964 Winter Olympics, though never used or put into production. Someone at the Leitz factory in Wetzlar, West Germany, apparently thought the lens might offer possibilities to a photographer shooting the Mexican Olympics during the summer of 1968. So, a couple of prototype lenses were sent to New York, en route to Mexico City.

It was one of these that I borrowed the day before I flew to Miami Beach to begin my NBC assignment. There, I suddenly discovered that I could have been shooting my desired closeups practically from Nassau—and free as an old jaybird from the other guys shooting around me.

The convention-floor lighting (balanced for television color cameras) gave me a basic exposure of 1/125 second at f/6.8 on Kodak Tri-X, which I used for every closeup tele-shot. The results—optically—astonished me, and still do. Of course, one question remains, regarding this fabulous 400. I wonder how sharp my negatives would have been had I stopped down?

My friends at Nikon in New York also rushed to my rescue with loans of an arsenal of Photomic-T Nikon F's, fitted with superfast lenses ranging from 24mm to 105mm—and extras, in case I got into real trouble in Chicago. Our friendship dates back to the Korean War. Nikon's directors knew what to expect. I had brought in from Khe Sanh a Nikon F with its 200mm telephoto, and two ancient M3D Leicas fitted with 21mm and 50mm lenses. So, with that borrowed new and battered old outfit, I headed for the two conventions—with four faded ammo-clip pouches on my belt for film—to shoot the big Stateside story for television and not a magazine. It seemed strange.

In Miami Beach and Chicago, other than trying to have a valid edit idea for each day's show and fighting off exhaustion that came with 20-hour work days (conceiving a story plan, shooting the story, printing and editing the pictures, *waiting* for the TV studio to be clear, filming and narrating the show—while going almost crazy watching the hour hand spin around with nothing yet in the box for the *next* day's show), I found that my greatest challenge was to forget—instantly—nearly everything I'd learned during a lifetime of shooting magazine-style, vertical full pages, and to start again, seeing life in the horizontal format of a TV tube—for almost every shot! Paradoxically, this vertical book was designed to accommodate the bulk of my horizontal, TV-format-designed photographs.

When Reuven Frank proposed the idea of producing a show a day from the presidential conventions—and I agreed—neither Reuven Frank of NBC, nor David Douglas Duncan of Castellaras, France, had the faintest clue what he was doing...that the whole project was suicidal. Maybe that's why it worked—at least, we thought so. All we had going for us was the fact that he was president of his network and could bulldoze a path for me through areas where I knew absolutely nothing about television—not even the far-famed taboos established by the various unions controlling all work within NBC's own studios. My qualifications were limited to being a professional loner accustomed to thinking editorially, and then producing my picture stories—good or bad—as highly distilled packages with little superfluous material clinging to the story-theme. Reuven Frank made it clear from the start that NBC wanted *my* viewpoint on the conventions—that, except for total technical support from himself and his network staff, it was, "Adiós, amigo—you're on your own!"

My first, obvious problem—even before having an edit idea of any consequence—was to provide for on-the-site, immediate, flawless photo-lab work...from undeveloped negatives to the finished enlargements, ready for the TV cameras. An old friend in *Life's* darkroom, Carmine Ercolano, offered to cancel his family summer vacation to help me during both conventions, fully aware he'd be working almost around the clock, each day. Late one afternoon, just before studio time, he made four 11 × 14 inch enlargements—perfectly matched for tonality—dried and mounted, in ten minutes! He did it unfailingly—there was no time for re-makes. My three-to-five-minute TV spots consumed from thirty to fifty photographs every day, with each enlargement balanced to the others—all necessarily of uniform contrast for television cameras. *That* took talent! The conventions finished, Carmine Ercolano reprinted every picture for this book—many never screened on my TV shows—working with me after finishing his night-shift printing at *Life*. We usually started around 12:30 A.M., folded at dawn.

Another good friend in New York, Miss Raysa Bonow, joined me for the two conventions as the assistant producer of my shows. Several years earlier, she had produced a TV-special based on my book *Yankee Nomad*, a film which revealed her awareness of what I had tried to say in that photographic autobiography. Her judgement of pictures was sensitive and ruthless: a fine editor.

Reuven Frank and NBC News provided the final three members of my TV unit. Mrs. Christie Basham, news desk coordina-

tor from their Washington bureau, brought an intimate knowledge of NBC's news operations, and a vast network of friends spread through all their units working the conventions. They gave her constant, invaluable research and information on the mercurial flow of events too widely flung to be within the immediate view of any single political correspondent. I was a convention novice, but Christie Basham's talent for providing me with precise background on all that was happening around us made my part of the assignment possible. There was no time to second-guess.

Reuven Frank also assigned two network experts to my unit: Marvin Einhorn as director, and Pat Trese as producer. Because of his familiarity with the technique of TV-camera movement across the face of a still photograph, Marvin Einhorn often gave my still pictures another dimension, a feeling of again being a fragment of our moving life scene. By panning, zooming slowly in for details, cutting, dissolving, and swinging cameras *against* the flow of motion in my original photographs, he imbued many of the televised images with separate moods of their own. One of the challenges in designing this book has been to retain that flow of action—with fixed images on a printed page. Pat Trese (associate producer of NBC's entire convention coverage) appeared each day, just before I put my pictures on TV camera to narrate "captions." Like everyone else, he worked with almost no sleep yet always found a way to guide me calmly through the foreign world of making a television show that was unrehearsed; one based entirely upon an inexperienced, extemporaneous narrator. No one, including DDD, knew what was going to be said on camera—something apparently unprecedented for a scheduled network television news show. Pat Trese acted as though it happened every day, but I'm sure he suffered moments of professional anguish, worried that I might inadvertently slip back into a former Marine's casual vernacular.

The whole darkroom crew of Vizmo—ultra-speed experts in making rear-screen projection slides for newscasters—shared their facilities with Carmine Ercolano: a dead duck without them! Then, there were those television-studio troopers, men behind TV cameras, on lights, men dropping my pictures into camera position, men who materialized before and after my shows—who passed along show-tips that had taken a lifetime to learn. And those rules-conscious television-studio unions? Not a man offered anything but help—as I broke their rules.

Again, my old Dutch friend in Haarlem—William Bitter, of Enschedé, with whom I manufactured *Yankee Nomad*—saved the production day by agreeing to print this book, deluxe format, deluxe gravure, at a cost that keeps it far below the sale price of "art books" of fewer pages, and of smaller format.

Many American publishers rejected this book as being quite impractical...too late...too lavish...too expensive. So now, I should like to thank Harry N. Abrams, who—knowing how other publishers felt—ignored the established program of his own art book firm to champion this work. His only comment, with a shrug: "The face of America is worth doing right."

Biographical Data: DDD

Born in Kansas City, Missouri, an archaeology major at the University of Arizona, and a graduate of the University of Miami (B.A. in zoology and Spanish), David Douglas Duncan has roamed the world since 1938 as a photographer, foreign correspondent, and art historian. He holds the rank of lieutenant colonel (retired) in the United States Marine Corps, where he was decorated with the Legion of Merit, Distinguished Flying Cross (2), Air Medal (4), and the Purple Heart.

During World War II, he photographed Marine Corps aviation operations throughout the Pacific, fought with the famed Fijian guerrillas behind enemy lines on Bougainville, filmed Marine fighter-bomber attacks against Japanese pillboxes on Okinawa (shooting pictures from inside a plexiglass-nosed capsule slung beneath the wing of a single-seat P-38 fighter plane). Duncan made the first landing upon the Japanese mainland and photographed surrender ceremonies aboard the *U.S.S. Missouri* in Tokyo Bay, then accompanied the initial Marine occupation force to enter Peking in the autumn of 1945—as China erupted in civil war between the Nationalists and the Communists.

In 1946, as a *Life* magazine photographer, Duncan took his cameras to Palestine, reporting from the center of terrorist battles between Jews and the British Army. In 1947, he was the only Western photographer to cover the Red Army take-over of Bulgaria. That summer, he stood in the middle of communal riots in India, where Hindus and Moslems were butchering each other. 1949 found David Duncan in war-torn Greece, recording the atrocities left in the wake of Communist efforts to conquer the Hellenic peninsula.

When the Korean War exploded in June, 1950, Duncan was there documenting the ordeal of the Marines on the Naktong river summer perimeter, and their December withdrawal from the freezing Chosin Reservoir. Duncan was the last man to be evacuated from Hungnam when the United Nations army was forced to abandon North Korea. He was awarded the *U.S. Camera* Gold Medal for his Korean War pictures. His book on Marines in combat, *This Is War!*, has been called by Edward Steichen "the greatest photographic document ever produced showing men in war."

In May, 1952, he took the first pictures showing the birth of the Iron Curtain in Europe (in 1947 he had made similar photographs disclosing the barbed-wire and machine-gun barricades raised by the Russians between Soviet Armenia and Turkey).

When Major General Mohammed Naguib and a young army colonel, Gamal Abdel Nasser, forced King Farouk to abdicate the throne of Egypt, in July, 1952, David Duncan photographed and wrote the story from inside coup headquarters in Cairo. For the next six months of 1952, he tracked Communist agents through western Europe, East Berlin, and East Vienna, proving they were purchasing embargoed strategic Western war matériel and shipping it to the Soviet Union. Throughout the spring and summer of 1953 he aimed his cameras at the French war in Asia, and predicted "Indo-China All But Lost"—nine months before the fall of Dienbienphu.

In 1956, having left *Life*, Duncan joined a multi-nationality volunteer force helping the Hungarian refugees fleeing Budapest. He worked with the Knights of Malta (without taking a picture), that Christmas and New Year, on the Austro-Hungarian frontier, his last contact with warfare until returning to Viet-Nam in the summer of 1967. Five of the years between wars were filled with photographing art subjects, and writing *The Private World of Pablo Picasso*, *The Kremlin and Its Treasures*, and *Picasso's Picassos*. Shortly before his 1967 assignment to Viet-Nam—after five years of work—he produced his word-and-picture autobiography, *Yankee Nomad*.

During his 1967–1968 trips to Viet-Nam, Duncan joined the Marines in their bunkers at Con Thien, on the DMZ, while the North Viet-Namese enemy tried to dislodge them with artillery fire. Later, Duncan was with other Marines in their besieged Khe Sanh outpost. His photographs of Con Thien, and Khe Sanh, were presented as television specials by the American Broadcasting Company. Simultaneously, they appeared as photographic essays in *Life* magazine; then worldwide. Shortly thereafter, Duncan's Khe Sanh coverage, pictures and text, became the book, *I Protest!* The Overseas Press Club awarded him its Robert Capa Gold Medal and the American Society of Magazine Photographers named him Photographer of the Year, for his 1967–1968 Viet-Nam reportage.